Beyond Coding

Beyond Coding

How Children Learn Human Values through Programming

Marina Umaschi Bers

The MIT Press

Cambridge, Massachusetts | London, England

The MIT Press would like to thank the anonymous peer reviewers who provided comments on drafts of this book. The generous work of academic experts is essential for establishing the authority and quality of our publications. We acknowledge with gratitude the contributions of these otherwise uncredited readers.

This book was set in ITC Stone Serif Std and ITC Stone Sans Std by New Best-set Typesetters Ltd. Printed and bound in the United States of America.

Library of Congress Cataloging-in-Publication Data

Names: Bers, Marina Umaschi, author.
Title: Beyond coding : how children learn human values through programming / Marina Umaschi Bers.
Description: Cambridge, Massachusetts : The MIT Press, 2022. | Includes bibliographical references.
Identifiers: LCCN 2021013278 | ISBN 9780262543323 (paperback)
Subjects: LCSH: Early childhood education—Computer-assisted instruction. | Computer programming—Study and teaching (Early childhood) | Computers and children. | Child development. | Values.
Classification: LCC LB1139.35.C64 B469 2022 | DDC 372.210285—dc23
LC record available at https://lccn.loc.gov/2021013278

10 9 8 7 6 5 4 3 2 1

"I believe in people. If I trust someone, we can work together to make our ideas concrete. But ideas cannot change anything themselves. They have to be shown to be true. And only people, living human beings, can do that."

Martin Buber (as told to Aubrey Hodes in *Encounter with Martin Buber*)

Contents

Acknowledgments

Gracias a la vida, que me ha dado tanto. "Thanks to life, which has given me so much" goes the song composed by Chilean Violeta Parra in 1966, just a year before she committed suicide. This song is beautifully performed by many, but my favorite version is by the Argentinean Mercedes Sosa, who made it into a personal anthem. In the United States, Joan Baez popularized it in 1974.

Gracias a la vida, que me ha dado tanto. This book tells the story of my intellectual journey. I started when I was a student of journalism and social communication sciences at the Universidad de Buenos Aires (UBA) as I first became interested in the communicative function of language. Later on, through my graduate work at the MIT Media Lab, I discovered the power of programming languages to think about who we are and the human values we cherish. During the last twenty years of teaching and doing scholarly research at Tufts University, I have worked with others to create new programming languages and support different forms of expression to develop computational thinking, coding skills, and character strengths.

In that journey, it is not only "life, which has given me so much" but also individual people: at the UBA, my professors, mentors, and friends, the late Aníbal Ford and Alejandro Piscitelli. Aníbal died several years ago, but I know he would have been proud of this work as he was a man of integrity. Alejandro is still active in his own research and teaching. For this book, through Zoom, we revisited old materials about the role of orality and literacy in society and discussed their relevance today. What a privilege to discuss this book with a mentor I gained when I was only twenty years old, thirty years later! *Gracias a la vida, Alejandro and Anibal, y Universidad de Buenos Aires.*

At the MIT Media Lab, the late Seymour Papert, Mitch Resnick, and Sherry Turkle played a very special role in my academic life. They taught me some of the most powerful ideas I ever encountered. Each one of them, in their uniqueness, supported my explorations, passions, and intellectual growth. Today, I am honored that one of my greatest mentors became a colleague. When in 2014 we launched ScratchJr, Mitch and I initiated together an adventure that impacts the lives of millions of young children all over the world. *Gracias a la vida, Seymour, Mitch, Sherry, y MIT.*

Rabbi Sergio Bergman has played a key role in my life. He is my rabbi, my teacher, my intellectual partner in new projects, and my friend. Throughout the years, we found different ways to work together and to engage in some of the most meaningful conversations of my life. As I started to write this book, Zoom conversations with Sergio helped me crystalized some of the harder ideas. *Gracias a la vida, Sergio.*

Over my two decades at Tufts University, so many people have inspired my work. In particular, I want to thank my colleagues Chris Rogers, from the Department of Mechanical Engineering, and Richard Lerner and Hanna Gebretensae from my own Eliot-Pearson Department of Child Study and Human Development, and Debbie Lee Kennan and Becky New, who are no longer at Tufts. All of them have been generous in discussing ideas, brainstorming projects, and teaching me about their own disciplines and methodologies. *Gracias a la vida, Tufts University.*

However, the biggest thank you at Tufts is for the wonderful students and staff at the DevTech Research Group. I started DevTech in 2001 as a brand-new assistant professor. Since then, the lab grew to over twenty people, an interdisciplinary group of committed undergraduate and graduate students, postdocs, staff, and research scientists working together to create the most amazing place to play and learn. It is at DevTech that the positive technological development (PTD) theoretical framework gets truly realized and the palette of virtues put in practice. None of the work I describe in this book could have been possible without the contributions of past and present DevTech members. In particular, for the preparation of this book, the following DevTech'ers helped me with different aspects: Megan Bennie, Melanie Becker, Riva Dhamala, Madhu Govind, Ziva Hassenfeld, Tess Levinson, Maya Morris, Emily Relkin, Amanda Strawhacker, Amanda Sullivan and Aim Unahalekhaka. Jessica Blake-West read and gave comments to the complete first draft. Laura De Ruiter suggested the paint by numbers metaphor. *Gracias a la vida, DevTech.*

At DevTech, we create prototypes and do research to improve them. However, to reach millions of children, we need products. I thank Mitch Rosenberg, who believed in my ideas and cofounded KinderLab Robotics with me in 2014. I also thank the wonderful team at KinderLab and its board members for making it possible for KIBO to reach thousands of homes and schools all over the world. *Gracias a la vida, KinderLab Robotics.*

Research needs money. Throughout the years, I have been fortunate to receive generous funding from the National Science Foundation, the Scratch Foundation, the Siegel Family Foundation, the David Lear Sulman Computing, Science, and Engineering Fund, and the Templeton Charity Foundation to support my work. *Gracias a la vida, foundations.*

My good friend Carey Schwartz graciously read and edited with a detail-oriented eye the manuscript several times and provided invaluable feedback on evenings at 9:00 p.m. sharp via email. Frank DeVito, one of the first friends I made when I moved to Boston, gave me thoughtful impressions based on his vast experience as an educator strongly grounded in the Catholic faith. Zvi Beckerman, from the Hebrew University of Jerusalem, reminded me of the relational aspect of any human activity. Mona Abo-Zena, from the University of Massachusetts Boston, discussed with me cultural funds of knowledge. My best friend from Argentina since I was a child, Vale Bakalar, a computer programmer herself, highlighted areas that were not clear, rejoiced at my stories, and confirmed their veracity. *Gracias a la vida, my friends.*

At home, my husband, Patricio (Pato) O'Donnell read the first complete draft and provided suggestions to clarify certain concepts and ideas for those, like him, who are not in the world of education. Pato's edits are just one more way in which he gives me the unconditional love and support that allows me to become a better person every day. Furthermore, as I watched him discover his new hobby of acrylic painting during the COVID-19 quarantine, the metaphor of a palette of virtues came to life. *Gracias a la vida, mi amor.*

My mother, Lydia Umaschi, who sent me to learn LOGO in Buenos Aires back in the 80s, is not only one of the smartest people I know but also, still, in her older years, a wonderful listener and intellectual partner. It was in conversation with her that the ideas in this book started to become clear and early drafts took shape. My dad, Héctor Umaschi, died in 2001, too young for his time, but he showed me, through his commitment to justice, how to live a meaningful life contributing to our communities. *Gracias a la vida, mami y papi.*

My children, Tali, Alan, and Nico, inspire me to repair the world and make it a better place. For many years, they have listened to my talks and contributed to my research by testing new technologies, providing feedback, and assisting in different tasks. As they grow, I grow with them. As they learn, I learn with them, and as they explore, I explore with them. It is in them that I see the palette of virtues coming to life. Tali, for whom coding is another language, inspires me with her kindness and sharpness. *Gracias a la vida, Tali.* Alan, thoughtful and insightful, challenges me to see the world in a different way. *Gracias a la vida, Alan.* Nico, hardworking and creative, teaches me about the mystery of the universe and suggested the title for the book. *Gracias a la vida, Nico.*

I want to thank Susan Buckley, from The MIT Press, for believing in this book and providing feedback to make it stronger. Finally, my deep gratitude to the thousands of children and early childhood educators, principals, and administrators, religious leaders, and researchers all over the world who have been part of this research over so many years and who have inspired me with their own palette of virtues.

Gracias a la vida, que me ha dado tanto.

Preface

It is March 30, 2020, and I am sitting with my computer in front of Mystic Lake in Massachusetts. Despite the beauty around me, my laptop is my connection to the world. During the pandemic, all my meetings happen online. And my teaching. And my social gatherings. And my shopping. And my yoga. Even my religious worship. We are navigating the COVID-19, or coronavirus, crisis. In the last few weeks, the world as we know it came to a close, slowly, country by country. The number of those infected, those who died, those who could not receive proper health care, and those in mandatory quarantine grows every day.

My screen became my window into humanity. I see creativity and need for connection, solidarity, and generosity. I see it in Winchester, my hometown in a suburb of Boston, and I see it in Buenos Aires, the place where I was born and raised. I see it when I speak with my friends and my family scattered around the world. It comes in different shapes and forms, according to unique cultural traditions. Musicians give concerts from their living rooms. Families in big cities go out on their balconies to clap in support of health professionals and essential workers. Some people chat with their neighbors for the first time. Others offer to go shopping for those at high risk. In some countries, the police and army enforce a "no one on the street" rule. In other places, people choose social distancing. Meanwhile, scientists and labs work around the clock on a vaccine. Engineers and factories struggle for efficient and cheap ways to make and distribute ventilators and tests. Immunologists and politicians map the curve and propose strategies to keep it as flat as possible.

As I write this book, it is obvious that both science and technology play a key role in how we respond to the coronavirus. So do our human values. These values guide our choices: staying home or going out, wearing a mask or leaving it at home, helping the elderly with groceries, or returning from the store as soon as possible. Today, more than ever, we are routinely faced with choices about how to live a good life. While hand washing is a personal choice, social distancing is not. It only works if everyone does it. The epidemiologist Jonathan Smith from Yale warns us on the radio station WBUR that "this unprecedented outbreak will not be overcome in grand, sweeping gesture, rather only by the collection of individual choices our community makes in the coming months. This virus is unforgiving to unwise choices." Science and technology are not enough. The pandemic of 2020, a transformational world event during which I started to write this book, reminds us of the importance of human values.

This book is about integrating the teaching and practicing of values with the learning of a programming language to express ourselves. As we engage in the process of creating our computational projects, we discover that values such as persistence, curiosity and generosity, open-mindedness, and forgiveness play an important role. In this book, much like the artist who works with a color palette, I offer a palette of virtues that shape the color of our process of learning to code. Programming becomes an opportunity for moral and ethical development as well as social and emotional growth. In this palette of virtues, I chose to place ten universal values, based on decades of observing the kinds of interactions, behaviors and attitudes happening in coding environments: curiosity, perseverance, patience, open-mindedness, optimism, honesty, fairness, generosity, gratitude, and forgiveness. Just as colors can be mixed to obtain new shades, new values can be added. Palettes change over time and colors morph. Different social contexts and cultures might have different palettes of virtues, but there is a universality to it. The metaphor of the palette of virtues reminds us that coding is not only a science but also an art produced by creativity and imagination, situated within the diversity of the human experience.

The ideas for this book started to emerge back in the early '90s. At the time, I was a student at the Universidad de Buenos Aires in Argentina. During the weekends, I served as a teacher in the religious school of my synagogue. I wanted to find better ways to teach young children about the core values of Judaism. I wanted to do more than just read traditional biblical stories and have conversations. Through my classes at the university, I learned about hypertexts and hypermedia. At the time, the World Wide Web was only for a handful of academics, and computers were not part of our daily lives. I developed a project called *"Genesis para armar"* ("Genesis to build up)." I was fascinated by the metaphor that the word creates the world, as it is portrayed in the Bible: "And God said, 'Let there be light,' and there was light" (Genesis 1:3). I wanted to explore how different cultural and religious traditions told the creation story.

I used HyperCard, one of the first hypermedia systems predating the World Wide Web, to create an application for the children at the synagogue to explore both science and religion, creation stories from different cultures and scientific explanations. With HyperCard, the children could find their own path to navigate existential questions and learn how to ask more questions. As I learned how to program, I realized that I was creating a world. For me, learning to code involved learning another language to express myself.

My journey into finding ways to integrate technology and identity, computer science and character development, and coding and human values continued in the United States during graduate school. My masters and doctoral work at the MIT Media Lab followed a similar path but using and creating more sophisticated technologies: virtual worlds and robotics. Later, during my tenure at Tufts University, I developed approaches and technologies for different age ranges. At the core of this intellectual journey is an obsession: leveraging the opportunities offered by new technologies to engage children in new ways of thinking, new ways of creating, and new ways to make themselves and the world better. I see the teaching of coding as an activity to explore, promote, and practice a palette of virtues that can change over time according to different cultures and contexts.

Before you start reading the book, I invite you to disconnect the learning of computer programming from STEM (science, technology, engineering, and math). I ask you to go back in time and remember when you first learned to read and write. You encountered a new symbolic system of representation. You discovered grammar and syntax. You realized that order matters in how you arrange letters in a word, words in a sentence, sentences in paragraphs, and paragraphs in narratives. You made mistakes, learned from them, and problem-solved. You marveled about the diversity of texts that can be created with only twenty-six letters in English or twenty-seven in Spanish. The first time you used written language to express yourself, to make a birthday card or to write a short story, you felt proud and shared it with others.

Slowly, over time, you learned to write your own complex narratives. You realized you have a unique story to tell. You also read other people's stories. You explored genres and interpreted what was not written explicitly but rather was conveyed through the text. In this process, you understood that reading and writing involve much more than the mechanics of coding and decoding. Literacy is a tool for expression and communication, for meaning-making and empowerment. That is the power of written languages, both natural and artificial.

When we use symbolic systems of representation, we can create or destroy worlds; we can build bridges or walls. Intention matters. It is the values we hold and cherish, our palette of virtues, that help us make choices. Learning how to program robots to move around, or to make animations dance on the screen, entails a cognitive activity, a socioemotional experience, and an opportunity for character development. The approach I describe in this book is not about teaching children how to code so that they become software developers. It is about children becoming future citizens who can think and act in new ways toward making the world a better place, about making explicit some of the implicit positive values hidden in the process of learning to code.

This is possible when we understand coding as another language, as a relational symbolic system that supports new ways of expression and communication. This book views coding as a literacy for the twenty-first century and proposes a pedagogy accordingly. Coding as Another Language (CAL) borrows strategies from alphabetic literacy to teach computer science. I focus on meaning-making and interpretation, expression and communication, dialogue and interaction. In this process, human relationships come to the forefront as well as the values, virtues, and character strengths that make them work. This approach focuses on coding but incorporates elements from a rich tradition grounded on moral education: using narratives to explore identity and values, developing logical thinking to think critically and to solve ethical problems, and having experiences in the community that enable the formation of personal relationships.

I hope you will enjoy the journey offered by this book and, as you read, explore your own palette of virtues.

1

Coding, Robotics, and Values

Pat (five years old): Look! My KIBO is flying!

Jeremy (five years old): It is not. You are making it fly.

Pat: I am pretending it is flying.

Jeremy: Your KIBO is not flying. You did not program it to fly. KIBO can't fly. You are just pretending.

Pat: So, what? It will land on your head.

On Tuesday August 1, 2017, the *New York Times* published a story about my work with robotics and young children. It described children's creativity and problem solving when programing our KIBO robots to dance the Hokey Pokey. The reporters narrated how five-year-old children learned to manage frustration when things did not work out. They wrote about children's persistence, determination, curiosity, generosity, and fairness, and they described how the children shared materials and helped each other. They quoted me saying "technology can be a vehicle to help people create and collaborate better, but at the end of the day, people need to learn how to work with people." I was proud to see my words chosen as the quotation of the day in this major newspaper. However, the heading of the story, in big, bold letters read as follows:

"Preparing Young Children for the Automated Economy." I was not happy.

The heading associated learning robotics with preparing the future workforce, and there is nothing wrong with that association. In fact, the jobs in information technology will grow 12.5 percent from 2014 to 2024, and robotics and automation will play a big role. However, for me, the heading emphasized the wrong thing. I do not teach robotics to a five-year-old so that she can find a job when she grows up. Learning robotics is much more than fulfilling the workplace pipeline. It is an opportunity to become critical thinkers, creative problem-solvers, communicators, and team players as well as to develop character strengths to make good choices and become a good person. It is an occasion to examine our values so that we can contribute to the making of strong communities. It is a good time for engaging with the ethical domain and not only the mastering of technical skills.

In the work I have been doing for the last twenty-five years with coding and education, I have found that the child's socioemotional and moral world grows alongside the cognitive dimension. I teach robotics to a five-year-old so that she can grow into a *mensch*, a Yiddish word describing a person of integrity and honor. If along the way her early exposure to coding and computational thinking helps her find a well-paying STEM job, that is wonderful. But that is not my goal.

Today, there is a growing push for bringing STEM education and robotics to schools all over the world. The focus is mostly on technical knowledge and skills. While those are important, cultivating character virtues alongside is crucial. This book provides a pedagogical roadmap that goes beyond STEM, which I call Coding as Another Language. Language is inherently social; it is about sharing information, stories, and ideas. It is about communication and interpretation. My choice to put the word *Coding* next to *Another Language* highlights creative expression, communication, and problem solving. It underscores that coding, when conceived as a language, situates us in the social world of relationships: with ourselves, with others, and with the world.

The philosopher Martin Buber, in his philosophy of dialogue, distinguished between I–Thou and I–It relationships that characterize the human existence as different kinds of encounters. In short, the I–Thou relationship stresses the mutual, holistic existence of two beings who engage in a dialogue, while the I–It relationship is nearly the opposite. The beings do not actually "meet," and one treats the other as an object to be used and experienced. Therefore, the I–It relationship is in fact a relationship with oneself; it is not a dialogue but a monologue. It is a transactional encounter. Buber argued that human life consists of an oscillation between I–Thou and I–It experiences and believed that the expansion of a purely analytic, material view of existence risked advancing I–It relationships, even between human beings.

My work hopes to highlight the I–Thou relationships, even in the context of learning how to manipulate the It, technologies. By focusing on learning to code as learning how to use an artificial language for expressive and communicative functions, this pedagogy not only situates the learning of programming as a new literacy for the twenty-first century but also as an opportunity for experimenting with I–Thou relationships that require us to treat ourselves, others, and the world with respect. In my perspective, this is one of the ultimate goals of education. We can get to know others and build bridges across language and racial barriers, cultural, and religious differences. It is in this process that we develop and practice our palette of virtues and learn how to find universal common ground within diversity.

The CAL approach involves much more than preparing students for STEM careers. It is about new ways of thinking, relating, and behaving. Literacy has the power to bring about social change and so does coding. Those who can produce digital technologies, and not just consume them, will create the democracies of tomorrow in an increasingly multicultural, multiethnic, and multireligious world. They will develop their own voices and grow up playing a role in both the economy and civic society. They will have the tools to innovate toward social justice and equity. They will understand that algorithms hide in our social media platforms and determine how the news, among other things, is presented to us. They will know that code determines rankings and can impact public opinion and will be aware of the racial and gender biases built into our algorithms. There is no doubt that they will have the technical knowledge to change the world. But they will also need character strengths and a moral compass to navigate the complexities of a global world in which universal values play with local contexts. The coding class, which I call a *coding playground*, can become another place to develop and practice them.

In this book I present four key ideas: coding as a playground, coding as another language, coding as a palette of virtues, and coding as a bridge. These ideas position the teaching and learning of computer programming as an opportunity to create I–Thou relationships. As you progress through the chapters, you will encounter them all. This chapter will explore the first idea, coding playgrounds, as environments that support open-ended discovery through the fun process of creating technology-rich projects to share with others. Coding playgrounds nurture I–Thou relationships by promoting cognitive, social, emotional, and ethical dimensions of the human experience. The next chapters, two and three, will provide the context in which computer science emerged as a discipline to be taught in schools and an overview of two very different pedagogical philosophies. Chapters four and five will investigate the second key idea, CAL, by exploring the relationships between alphabetical and digital literacies and practical approaches to bring it into the classroom. CAL is an integrated curriculum and pedagogy founded on a palette of virtues, described in chapter six, aimed at developing I–Thou relationships by working with technologies (the It).

The third key idea, coding as a palette of virtues, will be examined in chapter seven by presenting examples of how ethics and moral education might be infused into programming experiences at a very early age. Finally, the fourth idea, coding as a bridge, will be introduced in chapter eight as a new metaphor that puts forward the notion that, through programming, it is possible to provide opportunities for diverse cultural, ethnic, and religious groups to find points of connection, put assumptions and stereotypes behind them, and work together toward a common goal: learning to create personally meaningful computer-based projects that require coding skills.

Foundations: A Coding Playground

Young children are ready and eager to learn. They are curious and open to the world. They are creative sponges and have the needed cognitive and social structures to learn. Early childhood is a critical period. The brain develops rapidly and has a high capacity for change. These are the years when we must lay a foundation for health, well-being, and lifelong learning. However, we do not teach young children by lecturing them; it will not work. Children learn by playing. They play with numbers and letters, with objects and their bodies, and with rules and societal roles. They should also play with code. Then, our classroom can become a coding playground.

In this book, I advocate that in the coding playground, children can experiment with technical problem solving while also exploring values, virtues, and character strengths. The metaphor of a playground evokes playfulness in a social space. Children not only run around but also learn to negotiate and communicate. Conflicts are solved and ethical dilemmas arise. Should a child wait patiently in line for her turn on the seesaw or cut the line when no one is watching? Should she take over the sandbox and get rid of the castle with no owner in sight to build a bigger structure?

Not all experiences in the playground are the same. In this book, I explore how to create coding playgrounds in which I–Thou relationships can be nurtured, coding playgrounds that can serve to build bridges between those who are different and those who have no other shared language other than the programming language. Coding playgrounds in which children develop a palette of virtues useful for academic success and technical achievement as well as for being a mensch who understands responsibilities and consequences and who wants to make the world a better place.

Programming is a verb. It involves actions and not only thinking. Will the determination of a child who keeps debugging her program, even when outside recess is called, transform into grit in every aspect of her life? Can the generosity of a child who chooses to slow down and help another, instead of finishing his own robot as fast as possible, translate outside the coding playground? Can the creative ways in which children debug while coding transfer to solving social problems that impact equity and justice in the world? How about a child who chooses to share his KIBO robot with a child who has none instead of using it by himself? Will this child also display positive choices of conduct when faced with more complex decisions? In this book, I explore how to intentionally integrate opportunities for children to develop character strengths and to make choices about their behaviors into the teaching of computer programing.

I will use the terms *character strengths*, *values*, and *virtues* interchangeably. Although this book talks about coding, its focus is the human dimension. My intention is to offer an intellectual connection between the natural and the artificial symbolic systems of representation and between the cognitive and the social dimensions. In teaching coding, I see an opportunity to create I–Thou relationships, develop a palette of virtues, and put it to practice in the diversity of our experiences.

The CAL approach evokes alphabetical literacy. In the early years, literacy is an umbrella term that includes listening, speaking, reading, and writing as well as motivation, comprehension, vocabulary and socialization, and community participation. As children grow, they slowly learn how to comprehend and manipulate a symbolic system of representation—the written alphabet and punctuation. Reading and writing is not an isolated, one-year event in kindergarten but the result of multiple experiences that take place across many years in homes, childcare settings, and communities. Later on, schooling introduces literacy through formal instruction.

Our relationship with technology follows a similar path. While two-year-olds might learn how to use an iPad to find their favorite cartoons, it is doubtful they will be ready to navigate a complex interface. Neither will they create their own projects with a programming language. As children become developmentally ready, teaching can begin. As a pedagogy, CAL invites us to teach computer science by intentionally working with a palette of virtues that can be promoted in the coding playground. For now, the palette has ten values: curiosity, perseverance, patience, open-mindedness, optimism, honesty, fairness, generosity, gratitude, and forgiveness. Like the painter's palette in which new colors can be added, mixed, and matched, in this palette new values can be incorporated. While these values might be thought of as universal in the highly connected global world, different cultures, ethnicities and religions find their own ways to express, celebrate, and transmit them from generation to generation. They use their own words to describe them. They have their own sets of stories to illustrate the values in action. They develop their own rituals and practices to remember and celebrate them.

Programming languages also have a vocabulary of their own. Learning to code involves acquiring the syntax and the grammar of a particular language as well as the ways of thinking and behaving associated with the discipline of computer science. Problem solving, persistence, and open-mindedness are required to break a complex problem into simple processes; the disposition to work with others is necessary because programming involves working with a system created by another human being. The coding playground is an opportunity to put to use the values in our palette and further develop them. However, if the learning environment is solely focused on instrumental success and technical efficiency, or product over process, some of the values in our palette of virtues might go unexplored. I advocate that in early education, values are a priority. As children grow, they will have opportunities to develop efficient algorithms using sophisticated programing languages.

Languages for Children

We do not read Shakespeare in kindergarten nor do we ask children to write complex poetry. The same applies to coding; children need developmentally appropriate programming languages and age-appropriate projects. Back in 2007, when my children were young (Tali was seven, Alan was five, and Nico was three), I realized there were no programming languages for them. Scratch, developed by the Lifelong Kindergarten team led by my colleague Mitch Resnick at the MIT Media Lab, was designed for children eight and up. As wonderful as Scratch is, children need to know how to read and write. They also need a long attention span and a good working memory to not become overwhelmed by the large number of possibilities that Scratch offers.

That realization started a long-lasting research agenda for my DevTech research group at Tufts University. With colleagues and students, we designed and studied two introductory programming environments explicitly designed for young children aged four to seven: ScratchJr and KIBO.

ScratchJr was designed in collaboration with Mitch Resnick and the Playful Invention company and is currently used by over forty million young children all over the world. With an iPad or an android device, they can create animations, interactive collages, and games while learning how to program in expressive ways. Through generous funding from the National Science Foundation and the Scratch Foundation, we can offer ScratchJr for free.

The KIBO robot can be programmed with wooden blocks, without screens or keyboards. It was developed in my DevTech lab, with funding from the National Science Foundation, and is now commercialized by KinderLab Robotics, a company I cofounded in 2014 with Mitch Rosenberg, with funding from the National Science Foundation's Small Business Innovation Research program to make KIBO available all over the world. At the writing of this book, KIBO is available in sixty-four countries.

Both ScratchJr and KIBO are developmentally appropriate and engage children in a coding playground. However, technologies alone cannot change the way we teach. Thus, we also developed curriculum, teaching materials, assessments, and professional development strategies built upon the four foundational ideas in this book: coding as a playground, coding as another language, coding as a palette of virtues, and coding as a bridge. While technologies are likely to become obsolete sooner or later, ideas can have lasting power.

In my previous book, *Coding as a Playground*, I told the story of Liana, a five-year-old who proudly shared her ScratchJr animation with her kindergarten teacher. She had programmed the ScratchJr kitten to appear and disappear on the screen by putting together a long sequence of purple programming blocks. Liana cannot read yet, but she knows that these programming blocks can make her

ScratchJr kitten show and hide. Liana, like most children her age, wants to make the longest possible sequence, so she puts together ten blocks and screams, "Look at my cat! Look at my cat!"

Liana's kindergarten teacher walks over to see Liana's project. Liana is proud to show "my movie," as she calls it. Liana says, "I made it. Look at my cat. It appears and disappears, it appears and disappears, it appears and disappears. Many times. Look!" She clicks on the green flag on the ScratchJr interface, and the animation starts. Liana's teacher asks her, "How many times does the kitten show and hide?" "Ten times," replies Liana. "I ran out of room. I wanted more times." The teacher shows her a long orange programming block, called "repeat." This block allows for other blocks to be inserted inside its "loop." That way, Liana can make her program run for longer time despite the lack of space in her screen.

After some trial and error, during which Liana plays with inserting different combinations of the purple blocks inside the repeat block, she figures it out. She can put just one of each purple block (a show and a hide block) inside the repeat block and set the number of repetition times to the highest she can think of. She chooses the number ninety-nine and clicks the green flag to see the animation. The kitten starts appearing and disappearing. After a few seconds, she gets bored of watching. She goes back to her code and reduces the number of repetitions to twenty (figure 1.1).

During this playful experience, Liana engaged with powerful ideas of computer science that are accessible for a young child. She

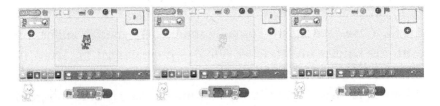

Figure 1.1
Liana's movie featuring the ScratchJr kitten animation

discovered the concept of loops and parameters. She also learned that a programing language has a vocabulary and syntax in which symbols represent actions. She understood that her choices had an impact on what was happening on the screen. She was able to create a sequence of programming blocks to represent a complex behavior (e.g., appearing and disappearing), used logic in a systematic way to correctly order the blocks in a sequence, and problem-solved when needed.

She practiced and applied the concept of patterns, which she had learned earlier in the year during math time. She engaged with mathematical ideas of estimation and number sense (i.e., ninety-nine is way longer than twenty). At the same time, she exercised her tenacity at tackling something she truly cared about (i.e., making a very long kitten movie). Liana created a project from her own original idea and turned it into a final product. She was proud to share it with others and happy to revise it when the final outcome did not meet her expectations (i.e., it ended up being so long that it was boring to watch).

All of this was possible because Liana's teacher integrated ScratchJr in a coding playground in which children had the freedom to make a project they cared about. Liana was excited and passionate. She was not going to give up until her cat did exactly what she wanted. She worked hard and rejoiced in that process, and she enjoyed learning and was fully engaged in it. For her, developing computational thinking involved more than problem solving; it meant gaining the concepts, skills, and habits of mind to express herself through coding.

A coding playground engages emotional and social domains as well as cognitive growth. Liana stuck to her project; she was persistent and debugged as needed because she truly cared about it. She felt proud and in control, and she wanted to share it. Her "cat movie" displayed an aspect of who she is: a five-year-old movie maker. Liana loves to watch animated movies and was thrilled to make her own. Through Liana's story, it is evident that programming languages such as ScratchJr provide a tool for expression. We need to learn their syntax and grammar, and over time, the more we engage with them, the more fluent we get. They become another language to us.

Coding does not only belong to the STEM disciplines. Similarly, the learning of a written language does not belong only to the language arts or English class. As an heir to Aristotle's philosophy and its logical systems, coding indeed engages children in critical thinking. This type of thinking belongs to every discipline and can be integrated into the general curriculum. Coding is for those who want to problem-solve technically and for those who want to problem-solve socially. Coding is for those searching new ways of expression and communication. Coding is for storytellers and engineers. Most of the dimensions of the human experience—the cognitive, the socioemotional, the language, the physical, the moral, and the spiritual—can be displayed and addressed by a well-designed coding playground, just like in the physical playground.

Starting Early

I first learned programming when I was ten years old back in the '80s. A renowned credit card company was running an after-school camp with the LOGO programming language in my home city, Buenos Aires, to promote their brand. My mother signed up both my brother and me. Twice a week, we went to a tall office building, sat in front of a computer, and learned how to make a little turtle on the screen draw a shape by moving up and down, putting its imaginary pen down, and choosing different colors.

I do not remember much about the experience except that it was difficult. I had a hard time thinking about left and right. It was confusing to draw the geometrical figures we were asked to do. A square required us to program the turtle to go forward first, and then turn right, and then go forward again, and then? I kept messing up. Which was my right? Was it the same as the right of the turtle on the screen? I needed to stand up and try things out with my own body.

Decades later, I would get to learn that Seymour Papert, the father of LOGO, had a name for that: *body-syntonic learning*. An example is a child pretending to be the turtle in order to learn. We can use our bodies and not only our heads to understand new ideas. I also did not know then Seymour Papert would become my doctoral advisor at MIT and that I would create my own introductory programming languages for children.

Although Papert became known as the pioneer of programming and education, his emphasis was never on the tools. He admonished us against a technocentric perspective that puts technology at center stage. His focus was on ideas. Papert wanted children to learn to think in new ways about all subjects and, most importantly, about the nature of thinking itself. He had worked with Jean Piaget before arriving to MIT to become codirector of the Artificial Intelligence Lab. With Piaget, he learned about cognitive development and "thinking about thinking."

I was inspired by Papert. However, I want children to not only think but to act as well. I want children to use those new ideas they encounter when programming to make the world a better place and themselves better human beings. I want them to be aware of their palette of virtues and put them to use. I want them to engage in I–Thou relationships and to understand the power of languages, both natural and artificial, for making them happen. We can create and destroy with them. The intention with which we use the language, and our guiding principles and values, make all the difference. CAL reminds us of this.

At the time when I was learning LOGO in Buenos Aires, most programming languages required reading and writing. It was impossible to think that a younger child could learn them. Today's interfaces do not need reading and writing. They can be block based, like ScratchJr, or tangible, like KIBO, so that we can start early.

We know that both economic and developmental reasons exist for teaching computer programming to children as early as possible, as long as it is done in developmentally appropriate ways. First, research in the neurobiological, behavioral, and social sciences extensively shows the importance of early life experiences. These impact brain development and human behavior, emotions, and social skills. Planned interventions and early educational experiences are crucial. Second, research by Nobel Laureate economist James J. Heckman and colleagues shows that early childhood programs can produce higher economic returns and are associated with lower costs and more durable effects than interventions that begin later on. Starting early is a good investment.

An influential report published in 2000 by the National Academies Press, "From Neurons to Neighborhoods: The Science of Early Childhood Development," alerts that "programs that enhance social and emotional development are just as important as those that enhance linguistic and cognitive competence." The approach I propose in this book taps into all of these components when bringing computer science to early childhood. Thus, it seems better suited than placing computer science as merely part of the STEM curriculum.

Of course, there are advantages to welcoming STEM. Research shows that when children are exposed to it at an early age, they demonstrate fewer gender-based stereotypes regarding STEM careers, increased interest in engineering and computer science, and fewer obstacles entering these fields later in life. Those arguments are important, but they reinforce the workforce pipeline. I have no problem with STEM education per se, and I welcome the addition of the arts into the STEAM acronym, but it limits the power of coding to a narrow group of disciplines and to the particular demands of the economy. It limits its power as a true literacy. Hopefully, after reading this book, you will be convinced of the power of coding as another language.

Starting early requires pedagogical strategies, curriculum, assessments, and programming languages that are developmentally appropriate for young children. It is not enough to copy or adapt what has been developed for older children. Creating models for younger children is the essence of my work. In my first book, *Blocks to Robots*, published in 2008, I wrote about how the development of new tangible interfaces that are age-appropriate for young children made it possible to introduce abstract computational concepts in very concrete ways. Papert, among others, had already argued that Piagetian stages could be questioned if children were given new intellectual tools. For example, a child does not need to understand the formal mathematical definition of randomness to see that when she uses a random variable in her program, there is an apparent lack of pattern or predictability.

A few years later, in my books *Designing Digital Experiences for Positive Youth Development* and *Coding as a Playground*, I used the metaphor of playgrounds versus playpens to explore pedagogical strategies. Coding can become a playground: an environment for us to be creative, to express ourselves, to explore alone and with others, to learn new skills and problem-solve while having fun. Playgrounds are open-ended, while playpens are limited. In a coding playground, children become producers, rather than just consumers, of digital artifacts that can be shared with others.

As children become producers of technology, they learn to master programming languages. Thus, I look carefully at what it means to use a symbolic system of representation, with its syntax and grammar, to produce an artifact that can be shared with others. However, the coding playground provides a learning experience that extends beyond coding and can intentionally promote the development of I–Thou relationships that reflect our human values.

I evoke written literacy, which for centuries has engaged people in the dialogical activity of meaning-making and interpretation through textual artifacts. Important lessons can be learned from experiences all over the world that see literacy as an opportunity for liberation, social justice, and equality as well as those who see literacy as imposing a colonialist set of values. If coding is to become the new literacy of the twenty-first century, what can we learn from the successes and failures of how this old literacy was taught? How can we design coding pedagogies and curriculum that take advantage of everything we know about teaching other symbolic systems of representation, such as textual literacy? How do we build on the power of artificial languages to bring people together, to learn about each other? How can coding serve to create bridges, not walls, in a global world that embraces diversity and pluralism?

I am concerned with character development, moral education, and ethics. Becoming a producer, learning how to use a programming language to create an artifact to share with others, means taking on a responsibility. First, it means we need responsibility with ourselves: working hard, persevering in the face of difficulty, and not giving up. It requires having a sense of excellence and acquiring the needed skills. Second, it means responsibility toward others: putting ourselves in their shoes, developing empathy, taking a different perspective, anticipating their reactions to our production, and making sure it is accessible and respectful. Becoming a producer also means accepting consequences: fixing what does not make sense and what breaks and anticipating that our creation might take on a different life when others make it their own. Last, it means understanding our responsibility toward the environment we are working with, the materials we are using and developing, and those we must learn to take care of. As you read the book, you will encounter all of these forms of responsibility described in the ten values I chose for my palette of virtues in the coding playground.

Responsibilities and consequences are the realm of both the humanities and the technical disciplines: literacy and STEM. This book describes a path for integration through eight chapters and a last section of recommendations for further readings and resources. Each of the chapters concludes with a vignette describing young children's experiences with coding and the role of the adults in the classroom. These stories help ground the discussion and provide a window into their world. Next, I present the first of these windows.

A Window into Their World: Mouths Cannot Read Bar Codes

Pauline is in kindergarten. Today, her teacher, Mrs. Payne, brought five orange robots to class called KIBO. According to Mrs. Payne, these robots can do many things, but they need someone to tell them what to do. They cannot think on their own and follow instructions. Pauline is not convinced. "How can we talk to them and tell them what to do? They will not understand us. They cannot hear us," says Pauline. "You will see," responds Mrs. Payne, "that there is a way of 'talking' to them. They 'understand' their own language. And we are going to learn it so that we can communicate with them. When we learn their language, we will become programmers." Pauline is confused. She always thought robots were smart, but now she must learn how to program them when they cannot even understand her.

Children sit down on their assigned spots on the classroom rug and make room for Mrs. Payne and her big box with the KIBO robots and colorful wooden blocks. Pauline is curious. Mrs. Payne explains to the children that they will learn the KIBO language, which is made of wooden blocks. "Take a look at all of these," Mrs. Payne says, inviting the children as she shows, one by one,

Figure 1.2
KIBO's programming blocks

the different blocks. "What do they have in common? What makes them different?"

Some of the blocks are blue, others are yellow, and there is a purple one. Some are cubes, and others are rectangles. They all have a peg on one side and a hole on the other, and they are meant to be connected to each other. After a more careful look, Pauline notices that not all of them have both a hole and a peg. There is a green block that only has a peg, and there is a red block that only has a hole (figure 1.2).

All of the blocks have a picture in the center, a word in English on the top, and a familiar image of multiple vertical lines of different depths. Pauline cannot read yet, but she recognizes the strange shape with multiple lines. She has seen it at the supermarket. "It is a bar code," shouts Carole. "When I go shopping with my mom, there is a machine that can tell you how much everything costs if you scan the bar code." The children nod. They have also seen it.

Mrs. Payne explains to her class that the KIBO robot has a scanner that can read the bar codes. "It looks like a mouth," adds Pauline. "No, mouths are red. This is made of plastic," responds Carl. "Mouths cannot read bar codes," shoots back Pauline. "If I press the button, there is a red light coming out of it. I think it is waking up the robot," contributes Carole. "I tried scanning the block, but nothing happened," she adds. The classroom becomes noisy with the excitement of different scanning strategies proposed by five-year-old children.

Mrs. Payne patiently explains to the children how in the KIBO language, the scanner can only read "sentences," not individual blocks. She calls these sentences *sequences*. She also explains that programmers like to use the word algorithm. She tells them that every sequence has to start with a green block and end with a red block. Those blocks signal to the KIBO scanner to start reading and to stop reading. "Like the red lights on the street," says Jasmine. "My dad stops driving when there is a red light and starts driving again when the green shows up." "Yes," adds Fermin, "like capital letters in a sentence and periods at the end. My sister is teaching me how to read."

Pauline volunteers to make the first sequence. She puts a blue block between the green and the red and scans all three blocks. Right before she is about to press the KIBO button to start, Mrs. Payne asks the class, "What do you think will happen?" "It will move," says Ron. "How do you know?" replies Mrs. Payne. "Because there is an arrow on the blue block," responds Pauline, who cannot read yet. "I know because the word says 'forward,'" adds Fermin.

Mrs. Payne explains to the class that the KIBO language is designed for different kinds of readers: those who know the alphabet in English and can read letters, like Fermin; those who can figure things out by looking at the symbols, the drawings on the block, like Pauline; and those who can scan the bar codes, like the KIBO robot. The students find this hilarious and start laughing. What follows is an engaging discussion about the many different languages spoken by children in that kindergarten classroom and the different alphabets that are used. Fermin shares that in his house they write in English, but in his grandparent's house they write in Spanish. He recognizes that the letters are mostly the same. Ron says that in his house, his parents use different letters. They come from Israel. Ron cannot read Hebrew or English, but he can see that the letters look different. Suddenly, the coding playground becomes a place to discuss culture and diversity.

Mrs. Payne stops the conversation and asks the children to program different sequences for KIBO. They make KIBO move forward and backward, turn its white light on and then its blue light on, and make it shake after someone claps and repeat forever a silly beep. They try different sensors, like the one shaped as an ear, that can "hear" a clap and do something, like shake.

This introductory KIBO lesson is designed to encourage children to think about programming languages in the context of natural languages. At this age, most five-year-old children do not know how to read or write yet, but they can recognize symbols. And they know that symbols stand for something else: meaning. After forty-five minutes of guided free play, children are ready to program silly moves for their KIBOs. Divided in small groups, they first need to decorate the robots with ribbons and colorful papers so that they can look even more silly (figure 1.3).

Designed with a playground approach, KIBO supports children in making almost anything: a character from a story, a dancer, a dog sled. The possibilities are endless, as wide as children's own imaginations. No computer, tablet, or other form of "screen time" is required to program with KIBO. This design choice is aligned with the American Academy of Pediatrics' recommendation to limit young children's exposure to screens.

Figure 1.3
A decorated KIBO

KIBO's programming language contains twenty-one different wooden blocks. Some of those blocks are simple, while others represent complex programming concepts including repeat loops, conditionals, and nesting statements. When we designed KIBO in the DevTech Research Group at Tufts University, we were inspired by a long tradition of using blocks and tangible manipulatives in early childhood.

Since the mid-nineteenth century, Froebel, Montessori, and others developed learning manipulatives to teach abstract concepts such as shapes, size, and colors. Many years later, Mitch Resnick extended that tradition by creating digital manipulatives to explore computational concepts. KIBO's design is inspired by this work and by tangible languages that use physical objects to represent the various aspects of computer programming.

Radia Perlman, a researcher at the MIT LOGO Lab, began experimenting with tangible programming languages as early as the mid-1970s. Since then, multiple tangible languages have been created around the world in which the physical properties of objects enforce syntax. For example, the KIBO begin block does not have a hole, only a peg, because there is nothing that can be placed before the beginning. The end block does not have a peg because there is no instruction that can go after the program ends. The language syntax in KIBO is designed to support and reinforce sequencing skills; its blocks can be sequentially connected in physical ways to each other. Learning how to sequence, understanding that order matters, is foundational in early childhood. It is needed for math, literacy, and most academic disciplines as well as for everyday life.

In addition to wooden blocks, the KIBO robot comes with sensors, motors, lightbulbs, a sound recording device, art platforms, and different extensions. For example, the expression module includes a whiteboard, markers, and flagpole so that children can make their own homemade flags, a Free Throw set with a catapult arm to explore physics and force, and a Marker Extension set that allows children to affix markers to KIBO's body to draw through code. This is one of my favorite modules, and it reminds me of the LOGO turtle and its different color pens. In Buenos Aires, I had a very hard time making geometrical shapes on the screen, but with KIBO on the floor, things are a lot easier. Of course, I am several decades older now.

2

The Coding Wars

Maria (five years old): My KIBO doesn't work.

Peter (five years old): Did you try new batteries?

Maria: No. I will debug first. It is missing a wheel.

Peter: Will that work?

Maria: I don't know. I will try.

It is 2018. I just finished giving a keynote in Lausanne, Switzerland, for the francophone community of computer science educators. There were researchers and teachers from Switzerland, France, Canada, Senegal, Ivory Coast, and a few other French-speaking countries. It was my first public talk in French, and I was exhausted. After the lecture, several people approached me. They had questions about computational thinking and wanted to know more about my coding as a playground metaphor.

As the conversations dwindled to an end, a tall man came closer. Behind him were fifteen or so girls, dressed in the same color t-shirts. They were all smiling. He explained that he is a teacher from a very small town in France and came to the conference with his students. The girls wanted to meet me, as I was their "hero." They loved ScratchJr and used it every day in his class. They wanted a photograph with me and also wanted to show me their ScratchJr projects.

Although I was ready to call it a day, I sat and invited them to join me. After the group picture, every girl, one by one, showed me her ScratchJr project. They were all the same! I was shocked. Gathering my best polite French, I commented, "These projects are interesting. How strange! All of them look exactly the same!" "Of course," replied the proud teacher, "I taught them well." He then proceeded to explain how he gave step-by-step instructions so that the girls knew exactly what to do. As a result, all of the projects looked the same. "I am very proud. In what other class can you have all students mastering the content so well?" he asked. I stuttered. Those fifteen identical ScratchJr projects represented what I had always fought against. ScratchJr, which we designed as a coding playground, had been converted into a playpen. Worse than that, it had become a factory that could produce identical copies of a project. Personal creativity was gone.

This encounter stayed with me for a long time. Back at Tufts, I talked about it in my classes and used it as an example of why pedagogy and curriculum are so important. The technology by itself is not enough, and even the best playground can be converted into a playpen. However, the teacher's attitude also remained with me: he was proud because all of his students mastered the content. I wished I had kept his email to ask him follow-up questions: Were these projects the first ones the girls programmed? What did he plan for them to do next? Were the girls engaged in this activity? Was this step-by-step instruction part of a bigger curricular unit?

My experience in Lausanne captures what I am naming the Coding Wars, in honor of a different kind of educational war, the Reading Wars, which started in the late '80s and has been raging for decades. While learning to talk is a natural process, learning how to read and code are not. People need to learn and need to be taught. The question is how. That is where the war starts, and two opposing camps emerge. One emphasizes teaching using step-by-step instructions, following a scope and sequence in a well-designed curriculum. The other, in sharp opposition, emphasizes learning by integration into meaningful activities following the development of the child and her active construction of an understanding. Both camps ground their pedagogies in research-based evidence. Like in any war, both sides have aspects that are right and both have aspects that are wrong. A balanced approach is usually needed, and CAL provides a middle way.

In the Reading Wars, academics, practitioners, and policymakers stand in opposing factions regarding how to teach reading. On the one side are those who champion "phonics" or letter-to-sound correspondence in a specific sequence so that children can learn to sound out words. On the other side is a focus on "whole language," or the meanings of written words embedded in text. Teachers provide a literacy rich environment for their students that combines speaking, listening, reading, and writing. Students are taught to use critical thinking strategies and context to guess the words they do not recognize.

The Reading Wars, like the Coding Wars, are research battles too. Academics on both camps propose different metrics for evaluating success, and these methodological differences often make it almost impossible to know who is right. The very essence of what is a good research question and how to answer it comes into play. Different views of the world are displayed when each side answers the "what" and "how" but also "why" it matters: the purpose of education.

In this chapter, I use the metaphor of the Coding Wars to tell a story about the confrontation between two opposing views on learning to program. On one side are instructionists and on the other are constructionists. The battleground: how to take advantage of the power of computation. As you read through the chapter, you will notice that I present an approach that, although is deeply grounded on constructionism, has elements of instruction.

The Two Sides: A Simplified Story

The simple story is this: instructionists focus on teaching and constructionists on learning. However, there is more to it. Instructionists draw from behavioral theories resulting from studies of animal behavior. In the 1930s, Harvard psychologist B.F. Skinner and colleagues conducted multiple experiments with rats. They found that rats learn to do tasks when they receive rewards in the form of food pellets. A behavior followed by a pleasant consequence is reinforced and likely to be repeated and a behavior followed by an unpleasant consequence is not. Extrinsic rewards, such as food pellets, play a key role in reinforcing the behavior. Behavioral theories informed the design of experimental studies with control groups to test the effectiveness of interventions for changing rats' behaviors and the behaviors of many others, including humans. Think about it: students receive a good grade as a reward for their high performance on a test, and this external reward might reinforce good study habits.

However, humans are not rats. It takes a little bit more than pellets or grades to change our learning behaviors. The process of education involves communication. However, the mechanisms and processes of communication are understood differently by instructionists and constructionists. Instructionists draw on the transmission model proposed by information theory in the mid-1940s. The mathematician Claude Shannon, the founder of information theory, studied the process of transmission of a message over a noisy channel. The goal was for the receiver to reconstruct the message with a low probability of error. In this linear model, the receiver is viewed as a target or end point, and she either successfully receives and understands the message or does not. It is the sender's responsibility to ensure the message is successfully transmitted and understood. Instructionists apply information theory to education, and thus instruction is very important. The channel is always noisy, and teachers need strategies to break communicative barriers so that the message can reach students without distortions.

Constructionists stand in sharp contrast. Knowledge is not transmitted like information in a pipeline; it is constructed by each individual. The sender has no control of how the message will be received. In contrast with the transmission model, instructionists describe communication as an interaction process in which participants alternate positions as senders and receivers. There is a feedback loop, and meaning is actively constructed. The focus is not on how to preserve the information itself (e.g., the message) in a noisy channel but on the interactive process of communication that creates new social forms, new information, and new knowledge.

In psychology, constructivist theories, such as those proposed by Jean Piaget and Lev Vygotsky, are aligned with this perspective. Furthermore, when coining the term *constructionism* for his philosophy on computers, learning, and children, Seymour Papert chose to capture the essence of "constructivism" with this new word. He replaced the "v" of constructivism with the "t" of constructionism. Although different in their approaches to cognitive development, both Piaget and Vygotsky understood children as active agents in the process of knowledge construction. In interacting with the physical and the social world, the reward that motivates learning is fundamentally intrinsic, feeling good about successfully accomplishing a task.

Full disclosure: I was trained in the constructionist camp. Papert, my mentor at MIT, had worked with Piaget and believed strongly that computers, and most explicitly the activity of programming, could help children develop new knowledge. Papert added a new dimension to Piagetian stage theory. He proposed that when programming with tools such as LOGO, children could engage with abstract ideas in very concrete ways. For example, while a nine-year-old cannot recite the mathematical function that makes a triangle, she can draw one with turtle LOGO and construct a personal understanding of angles.

Although there is no formal war between instructionists and constructionists, the pedagogies and the teaching materials, as well as the research studies and methodologies, often reflect opposing views on the process of teaching and learning. Instructionists and constructionists think differently about the role of the teacher and the student in this process, the role of education in society, and even the reasons why coding is taught. However, much like in the Reading Wars, extremes never win. Only a balanced approach can integrate best practices.

The Role of the Teacher

Instructionists favor explicit teaching. The "sage in the stage" decides what, where, when, and why to teach. The teacher follows a planned sequence in the curriculum, and the scope is decided a priori, based on the core content and skills of the discipline and the mandated policies. Although the teaching of computer science and the available programming languages changes over the years, problem solving remains at the core. The teacher presents problems or challenges, and children solve them using taught strategies. As they learn more, the problems become more difficult. The teacher makes the instruction accessible to students according to their ability and their prior knowledge. In this teacher-centric model, the teacher rewards students and gets them ready for the next level. An experienced teacher can judge the student's understanding and engagement and adjust the transmission of the message.

Most of my teachers in elementary and high school were instructionists, and some were better than others. There was a syllabus with a scope and sequence of the content to be covered and daily lessons. The teacher was at the front of the room, writing on the black board with white chalk while we all sat in neat rows. Some teachers were fun and engaging; they could capture our attention with their stories and were master entertainers. Others were oblivious to our moods. They repeated their lessons by heart. At the end of the year, there was a test, and based on the outcomes, students could move up a grade or repeat it.

In kindergarten there wasn't a neat row of seats, but the teacher was still at the front. Small round tables with four or five little chairs populated the classroom. The teacher would read a story out loud, and we all had to draw what we heard. We had to copy the shapes of letters in our notebooks, making sure we did not go over the dotted lines. We all sang the same song during music time. Although play was a big part of my kindergarten classroom experience, that was not considered instruction. That was play time.

In contrast, constructionists embrace play and emergent curriculum as part of the learning process. Papert, the father of constructionism, refused to give a concrete definition. In 1991, he wrote that "it would be particularly oxymoronic to convey the idea of constructionism through a definition since, after all, constructionism boils down to demanding that everything be understood by being constructed." He believed in learning much more than in teaching. Constructionists set up environments for children to bring their own passion into learning, to discover, to invent, and, while doing so, to encounter new powerful ideas.

Those ideas might not follow a neat sequence. There is not a priori curriculum, and instead the curriculum emerges based on the child's needs and interests. The teacher becomes a coach, a guide to help children explore their passions and to ask new questions. The teacher's job is to meet the students where they are and to offer a rich environment based on the changing and evolving interests of the child. They provide "just in time" guidance. In other words, the less teaching, the better. For constructionists, problem solving in computer science is not a goal in itself but a means to create personally meaningful projects. Teachers do not offer challenges; they present a theme to explore. Children find the challenges on their own as they embark on projects of their choice. All projects in a classroom look different from each other because all children are different and so are their passions.

Back in the late '90s, when I was a doctoral student at the MIT Media Lab, the internal joke was that Papert did not come with LOGO to schools. What we meant was that although we were bringing LOGO to classrooms, many teachers used LOGO in instructionist ways; they did not incorporate Papert's pedagogy. Creativity and personal expression were left out.

The Coding Wars narrative oversimplifies the role of the teacher in the education process. However, by making a caricature of the two extremes, I am able to highlight the differences. Although I was trained as a constructionist, through experience, I realized we must adopt a flexible approach that is responsive to student needs, passions, and ideas and, at the same time, provides equal opportunities for every child. In a nutshell, that is a curriculum. A well-designed curriculum supports teachers to notice and ask questions, plan in advance and improvise, use the classroom as a site of inquiry, experiment with different teaching interventions, take risks, and provide scaffolded opportunities for students to encounter new powerful ideas. In this process, both teachers and children become agents of their own learning.

The Role of the Student

Instructionists believe that students should follow instructions. If the student pays attention and the teacher is a good instructor, the result will be positive. This approach emphasizes product over process. As long as the student can produce the desired outcomes, she will be rewarded. The grading system, as we know it, is based on an instructionist mindset. The student receives the instruction, performs the test (which is often multiple choice and hides the student's thinking that led to the chosen answer), and is rewarded with a grade. The student is passive, and the motivation is external. Depending on the student's cognitive resources, she might use rote memorization, visual learning, auditory cues, and so on. This student is contributing little, if anything, to the instruction process. She receives what the teacher gives her and, if needed, can ask for clarifications.

The girls in Lausanne who showed me their identical ScratchJr projects appeared to be happy, proud, and motivated. The teacher was an engaging man. For all of them, instructionism seemed to work. These girls were socialized in a school culture in which every student does the same thing. In French class, they copy the same poem from the white board. In math, they solve the same problem using the same strategies. Coding class was not different. Girls knew what to expect and so did the teacher. These girls were lucky because they had an engaging teacher. This teacher was also lucky, as sometimes there are students who cannot follow. That is when instructionism breaks down.

When I was ten years old learning LOGO in Argentina, I failed miserably as an instructionist student. I did not understand angles and could not follow the teacher's instructions. Despite my good attitude, I could not program the turtle to draw the geometrical shapes the teacher wanted. Instead, strange looking triangles and messy shapes showed up on my screen. I was not proud of those creations. In my mind, I was a failure. I was not able to do what I was told and felt like there might be something wrong with me.

In a constructionist environment, my role as a student would have been conceived differently. My identity as a learner also would have been different. The teacher might have encouraged me to make my own geometric shapes. She would have invited me to explore their differences and similarities. She would have asked me questions, and based on those, she would have challenged me to make new shapes. She would have celebrated my unique contributions to the class and might have even asked me to share them with others. Together, as a class, we would have explored my shapes.

What was special about my angles? How many steps did my turtle move forward after turning? Could I teach the class how to make such strange shapes? My teacher would have taught me the names of those shapes, and I would have learned something new. I would not have followed a scope and sequence that determines which shapes should be learned first, but in the end, I would have learned them all. And most importantly, I would have felt proud of myself as a learner.

Constructionists see the child as an active learner in charge of choosing what she wants to learn and how. The child needs to be internally motivated because there is no external reward waiting. If the tasks and projects are sufficiently authentic and meaningful, the child's motivation would be high and she would want to learn. She will do well if given the opportunity to create self-directed independent projects based on her own interests.

Decades after my failed LOGO experience in Argentina, I took my favorite class at the MIT Media Lab. It was 1994 and the class was Mitch Resnick's Technological Tools for Learning. During one of our first meetings, I was asked to make any project I wanted with LOGO. Fear immediately swept me. I remembered that I was not able to program perfect triangles. The fact that I was now a twenty-four-year-old taking graduate classes at MIT did not matter. My mind went straight to my first painful experience with LOGO.

However, Resnick's class was different. Having been a student of Papert, Resnick set up his class in such a way that students could be in charge of their own learning. I could create any project I wanted. For the next few hours, I programmed two turtles to dance tango, avoiding the triangles. To dance, I programmed the turtles to trace figure eights. Despite my initial fear of failure, I loved the project.

I loved LOGO and loved programming. I had a story to tell and wanted to share with my classmates my favorite dance, the tango. In the process, I explored the hidden geometry. This experience worked for me, and I was motivated to succeed at MIT. However, sometimes children grow so out of touch of what motivates them that it is hard to tap into it. It takes time, patience, mentoring and scaffolding.

At opposite sides of the Coding Wars, both instructionists and constructionists fall into a similar trap. Despite the role of the teacher, children's experiences are as varied as their diverse socioeconomic, racial, linguistic and cultural contexts. For some children, to be part of a reward system, such as getting a good grade, might be perceived as reinforcing unequal traditional societal roles. For others, achievement within the system is the goal. Some may place greater emphasis on group or family expressions of achievement and approval. In addition, children from different social classes and ethnic backgrounds come to school differently prepared by their home and preschool experiences and by their parents' involvement, values, aspirations, and motivations. For example, there are consistent findings that show that the higher the family's social status, the more likely the child is to have high scores on achievement tests.

The Anglo-American definition of achievement motivation based on individualistic achievement efforts might not work with children from different racial or ethnic groups. Children enter school with different capacities and levels of preparation as well as culturally different socialization goals and experiences. We know that the schooling experience varies for different socioeconomic backgrounds. Even when students live in comparable neighborhoods, home environment is still a variable. And if everything in the environment is equal, physical growth, cognitive, and socioemotional maturation still cause inevitable differences in learning. Children do not develop following an exact path or timeline.

Furthermore, while some children learn best in structured environments, others need to find personal meaning. Each child is different. The challenges of having to define, a priori, the role of the child in the educational system are many. The child becomes an object of the educational system and stops being a subject. In Martin Buber's terms, the I–Thou relationship becomes I–It. Who is this individual? What does she need at this time? What motivates her? If instructionists and constructionists come to the teaching and learning process without asking these questions, the real outcome of this process, the child, risks being ignored.

Just like in any other academic war, the Coding Wars need balance: an active role for the child in guiding the learning process, presence of diverse curricular materials to stimulate student exploration and learning, a combination of group and individualized instruction, a scope and sequence of what needs to be taught, a teacher's flexibility to achieve those goals, and diagnostic iterative evaluation to assess the learning process. Without all of these components, it is easy to lose sight of the end goal: to educate our children.

The Role of Education

Instructionists and constructionists agree that schools must provide opportunities to develop cognitive and socioemotional competencies as well as to serve other less obvious societal functions: childcare while parents work or pursue personal interests; maintain established social roles, power dynamics, and institutions; and delay children's entrance into the workforce.

Instructionists see the role of education, and therefore schools, to impart knowledge and skills so that learners can participate successfully in society's institutions. Thus, according to instructionists, in a globalized world in which technology is having a growing impact in every area, the teaching of coding must fulfill the needs of society: workforce development and a pipeline for growing STEM careers. Every school needs to have "an hour of code," at a minimum, so that all students can be exposed to this new skill. If students like it, then they might consider taking a course later on and even contemplate a technical career. The needs of the economy will be met, and education will have played its part. School is the official institution that ministers education, and as such coding needs to be included in the coursework.

In contrast, constructionists focus on individual development. According to constructionists, the role of education is to foster independence and a sense of personal power to express ourselves. Children need to discover their own passions, and learning to code can bring a sense of empowerment by making those passions come alive. The role of education is to support that process by helping and guiding children in this individual pursuit. Papert wrote that "if you love what you learn, you'll get to love yourself more. And that has to be the goal of education, that each individual will come out with a sense of personal self-respect, empowerment, and love for oneself, because from that grow all the other loves: for people, for knowledge, for the society in which you live."

Constructionists do not always see schools as the most likely place where education happens. Quite the opposite. There is extensive writing on how schools might damage learning by forcing everyone to learn the same things at the same time. Furthermore, in its earlier days, constructionists aligned with some of the ideas of the deschooling society movement proposed by Ivan Illich and others. Illich wrote that "equal educational opportunity is, indeed, both a desirable and a feasible goal, but to equate this with obligatory schooling is to confuse salvation with the Church." Ahead of his time, back in the early '70s, Illich saw technology as an opportunity for deschooling society through the formation of what he called "learning webs." These webs would "provide all who want to learn with access to available resources at any time in their lives; empower all who want to share what they know to find those who want to learn it from them; and, finally, furnish all who want to present an issue to the public with the opportunity to make their challenge known." As we read this today, we of course think about the internet.

Constructionists also saw the power of learning webs to spark more authentic learning experiences than schools. Learning webs could help form communities of practice, people engaged in a process of collective learning in a shared domain. Papert used the example of Rio de Janeiro's *escolas de samba* (samba schools) to describe an ideal learning setting. He wrote the following:

> A very remarkable aspect of the Samba School is the presence in one place of people engaged in a common activity—dancing—at all levels of competence from beginning children who seem scarcely yet able to talk, to superstars who would not be put to shame by the soloists of dance companies anywhere in the world. The fact of being together would in itself be "educational" for the beginners; but what is more deeply so is the degree of interaction between dancers of different levels of competence. From time to time a dancer will gather a group of others to work together on some technical aspect; the life of the group might be ten minutes or half an hour, its average age five or twenty-five, its mode of operation might be highly didactic or more simply a chance to interact with a more advanced dancer. The details are not important: what counts is the weaving of education into the larger, richer cultural-social experience of the Samba School.

Samba schools or traditional schools present a different perspective on education's role in society. While constructionists hope for the apprenticeship model of the samba school to replace the current structure and function of schools, instructionists want to work with the existing educational system to bring about pedagogical reform. For both, the introduction of coding is an opportunity to bring about change and engage in the reenvisioning of policies and institutional decision making.

However, we must avoid what Papert called *technocentrism*. Papert, who loved to play with words, borrowed this term from Piaget's egocentrism: "This does not imply that children are selfish, but simply means that when a child thinks, all questions are referred to the self, to the ego. Technocentrism is the fallacy of referring all questions to the technology."

Will coding have this or that effect on the schooling experience? Will the learning of computer science improve mathematics or literacy outcomes? Will it increase children's creativity and interpersonal skills? Or will it lead to isolation of children from one another? All of these questions reflect technocentric thinking. No single content area or skill is powerful enough to restructure the way we think about schools and the role of education in society. The how, when, and why we teach coding and computational thinking reflect deeper issues of educational theory, policy, and philosophy. Education occurs in the context of society at large, and schools' functions are not independent of other societal institutions and power structures.

I believe that Papert asked relevant questions that are central to the ideas I am presenting in this book: "What kind of people, what kind of citizens, do we want? Do we want empowered individuals who will feel the power to make their own decisions and to shape their lives? Or do we prefer citizens who will accept the discipline of following the instructions and the programs that are set up for them by others?" I find these questions useful for thinking about education in general and most specifically about why and how we teach coding.

The Role of Coding

Instructionists and constructionists agree on the importance of teaching computer science starting early on. However, in my opinion, the rationale is slightly different. Instructionists see coding as a needed skill set for a future that will require a highly trained technical workforce. Coding knowledge will be a must in the job market. This perspective might be problematic in early childhood. Is it developmentally appropriate to advocate teaching coding to five-year-old children so that they can have a job in the future? Instructionists might respond yes because computer science is not merely for computer scientists anymore. It permeates every discipline, and thus we need to teach it as soon as possible. The challenge is how to instruct in a developmentally appropriate way.

In contrast, constructionists see coding as a new way of thinking, beyond workforce preparation. Building upon the Piagetian legacy, Papert and colleagues focus on intellectual growth. When coding, children encounter powerful ideas from computer science, such as algorithms, representation, control structures, and modularity. These ideas are personally useful, epistemologically interconnected with multiple disciplines, and have roots in intuitive knowledge that a child has already internalized over a long period of time. For example, an algorithm is a sequence of actions that serves to both instruct a robot what to do but also tells a cook how to follow a recipe. In early childhood, understanding algorithms requires comprehending sequencing and that order matters. This logical way of thinking is foundational for later academic success, such as setting the building blocks of math and literacy. It is also important for recognizing that when getting dressed in the winter mornings, boots come after pants.

Instructionists and constructionists agree that coding engages children in a new way of thinking. However, the question is how to teach it. In early childhood, it is often the case that instructionists teach coding through computer games and puzzles. Children progress through problem-solving levels in a sequenced instruction with rewards. For example, in Code.org's Classic Maze game, children write lines of code in a setting inspired by a popular game to

Figure 2.1
Screenshot of level 1 of the Classic Maze game on Code.org

help the angry birds get to the naughty pigs (figure 2.1). Each level makes it increasingly more difficult to navigate to the pigs, as new concepts are introduced with new tasks and rewards. These kinds of sequenced games can be effectively used worldwide, even when there are not enough trained teachers to teach computer science to children. As evidenced by the success of the Hour of Code global movement that has reached tens of millions of students with over 500+ one-hour tutorials and is available in over forty-five languages, instructionist types of experiences can promote a democratization of computer science education.

Constructionists view these types of games as limiting. They are playpens that offer a narrow set of experiences. While they focus on computer science and problem solving, they do not support children in the process of creating their own meaningful projects. In contrast, coding playgrounds, such as ScratchJr, are open-ended and promote child-directed exploration and the creation of projects that express the child's unique interests and individuality. Inspired by a long-lasting tradition of constructionist programming languages, such as LOGO and Scratch, with ScratchJr, children learn by experimenting and by making mistakes, fixing their bugs, problem solving, and encountering powerful ideas from computer science.

Figure 2.2
Screenshot of the ScratchJr interface

As an introductory programming language, ScratchJr provides developmentally appropriate blocks, spanning from simple
sequencing to control structures. When children put them together
as a jigsaw puzzle, they can control their character's actions on
the screen (figure 2.2). As children create their ScratchJr projects,
they learn how to use a symbolic system of representation to make
a sharable product that others can interpret. In the process, both
problem solving and personal expression emerge.

ScratchJr is a playground; the Classic Maze game is a playpen.
The *playground versus playpen* metaphor that I coined in my previous work describes the preferences that constructionists and
instructionists choose when introducing programming and computational thinking. Coding playgrounds invite open-ended imagination and creativity. They require time to fully explore and enjoy
them. In contrast, coding playpens can be visited during a short
period of time, but there is less freedom to experiment and explore.

Although playpens are goal directed and safer, playgrounds support infinite possibilities. In the coding playground, social interactions are important. I–Thou relationships can be nurtured and sustained; learning involves humans working with humans. In the coding playpens, instead, sophisticated artificial intelligence algorithms might be enough.

As a designer of coding playgrounds for young children, I am clearly in the constructionist camp of the Coding Wars. Inspired by the work of Papert and Resnick, tools such as ScratchJr and KIBO robotics engage children in the making of creative projects and learning communities. In the process, they learn new skills and journey through the design process from an early idea to a final sharable product. They learn how to manage frustration and how to persevere toward finding a solution rather than giving up when things get challenging. They fail and start all over again, and they develop a muscle for forgiving their own mistakes and those of others. They come up with strategies for debugging and fixing their projects. They grow optimistic in their ability to be open-minded and flexible in trying different approaches. They learn to collaborate with others, are generous in helping each other, and grow proud of their hard work. They develop their own palette of virtues.

A Window into Their World: Robotics Guarding Nature

A kindergarten public classroom in Buenos Aires, Argentina, has been exploring environmentalism for several weeks. They have read books and learned about how to take care of our environment. They created a list of doable actions at home, school, and the neighborhood. They explored different habitats and discovered what is needed to keep them healthy. They learned that plastic trash is bad in every habitat but in the ocean it can also hurt fish. They also made drawings and watched documentaries.

One day, Malena, the teacher, brought a surprise: several KIBO robots. The children were excited. They had seen robots in popular movies and were eager to share their knowledge. Marcos saw a video clip of a robot that explored Mars. Julia's aunt bought a robot vacuum cleaner. Sofia told the class how her father, a surgeon, uses robots in his work. After a discussion centered on what is and what is not a robot, Malena explained to the eager five-year-olds that the KIBOs she brought were now their classroom robots. She showed how to program them with wooden blocks and how to use the art platforms to decorate them.

Some children were deeply disappointed. They expected KIBO to be big and smart and to "look more like a robot." Others were excited because KIBO has an art platform "and we can make it look the way we want." "Exactly!" responded Malena. "We will transform the KIBOs into our 'guardians of nature.' and we will program them to go around the classroom cleaning up our environment. But first we will use these posters to represent our environment. We will draw the different habitats that we have been studying."

Students were divided into groups and slowly started making oceans, mountains, lakes, and cities on big posters. Malena walked around the room with plastic bottles, cups, and other 3D materials to represent trash and slowly spread all of them in the different poster environments drawn by the children. "Now," she said, clapping her hands three times to get the children's attention, "We will program our KIBOs to go around the room and stop when they find something that needs to be cleaned up."

The classroom liked the challenge. Divided into groups, the children came up with different strategies to program their KIBOs to know when to stop and clean up. A group decided that KIBO needed the help of superpowers to do a better job and drew a superhero to sit on KIBO's back. Some children counted the steps from one spot to the other and hardcoded KIBO to travel from trash to trash. This strategy posed a problem when a distracted child would kick the trash and move it to another spot. Other groups used the clap sensor to avoid this issue. A child would program KIBO to go forward forever and stop when it heard a clap, and another child was designated as the clapper and would follow KIBO around. When it encountered trash, she would clap so that KIBO would know when to stop. This strategy also had its limitations in a noisy classroom.

Creativity and laughter abounded in Malena's class. The children were drawing and programming, counting steps, and exploring different strategies. They were creating long sequences and debugging them. Conversations about nature, ethics, and robots were loud as the children worked with others and problem-solved together. There was lots of trial and error and children running around. It was hard to tell it was robotics time and not a playground.

3

The Rise of STEM

Andy (seven years old): Let's make the cat run a race with the fish. He can win. I will program it to win.

Clara (six years old): I don't want to. Can we make them go to the park?

Andy: It is boring. Let's make them race. The cat can jump up and down after he wins.

Clara: No.

Andy: Ok. I will make them race to the park.

It is 1992. I am living in Buenos Aires, Argentina, and I am excited. I cannot wait to tell my dad that Seymour Papert has finally answered my questions. As a junior journalist, I was working on a story about him for the *Uno Mismo* magazine and had sent him an email with follow-up questions. Day after day, I would go to the only office that had a computer with email access to check if Papert had responded. My mentor, Alejandro Piscitelli, gave me an account and let me use his computer. At the time, I did not have an email account or connectivity of any kind, like most people around the world. After a few weeks of checking, Papert's response was finally in my inbox. Piscitelli printed it out for me, and I ran home.

I found my dad sitting at the dinner table, watching a soccer game. I turned off the television and showed him the printed email. My dad, who did not speak English and could not understand the words, saw my enthusiasm. I translated for him and explained that I wanted to study with Papert at MIT in Boston. I told him that I was captivated by Papert's ideas. My dad looked at me with a sarcastic grin and asked, "You do not like math, or science, or technology! What is so thrilling about programming?"

My dad's question evokes the widespread association between STEM and coding. In the United States, the history of this connection can be traced back to October 4, 1957, when the Soviet Union launched Sputnik I. The world's first artificial satellite was small, the size of a beach ball, and not very heavy, only 83.6 kilograms or 183.9 pounds. However, in the midst of the Cold War, Sputnik I changed the power play between the United States and the Soviet Union. In addition, and more relevant to this book, it brought about educational changes to improve the technical skills of the workforce and to protect national security.

Sputnik took about ninety-eight minutes to orbit the earth on its elliptical path. In the process, it transmitted radio signals that could be picked up by amateur radio operators. The Sputnik launch caught the world's attention and stood as a symbol of the technical and scientific achievements by the Soviet Union that surpassed the United States. On November 3, 1957, Sputnik II was launched. It carried a much heavier load, including a dog named Laika. Fear about the capability of the Soviets to also launch ballistic missiles with nuclear weapons started to spread. In response, the US Department of Defense approved new funding for a US satellite. The space race began.

A few months later, the United States successfully launched Explorer. In addition, two federal agencies were created: the National Aeronautics and Space Administration (NASA) and the Advanced Research Projects Agency (later renamed the Defense Advanced

Research Projects Agency, or DARPA). It took almost ten years, with the Apollo lunar landing program, for the United States to take a giant leap and land two astronauts on the moon's surface in July 1969.

The realization of the need to improve the technical workforce had positive consequences for education. In September 1958, the US Congress enacted the National Defense Education Act (NDEA) with the goal to grow the workforce and maintain national security. While the NDEA covered many areas of education, it has been credited with an emphasis on increasing the number and quality of US scientists and engineers. This policy marked the federal commitment to disciplines that we now group under the STEM acronym.

At the time, the NDEA provided funding and incentives for all levels of the American school system to improve—among other subjects—math, science, and engineering, as well as modern foreign language curricula. The underlying rationale was that other languages beyond English were needed to conduct foreign policy and to help US businesses expand into international markets. The NDEA did not identify or promote the teaching of computer science, as the role of computers and programming was limited at the time. With the rapid growth of digital technologies in everyday life, however, this has changed.

Cultivating a high-tech workforce involves a long educational process and a pipeline that starts in early elementary school and sustains itself through high school and college. The story of the space race between the United States and the Soviet Union is tightly linked to the story of how computer science came to be included in K–12 American education. Throughout different historical periods, the STEM acronym went through variations in the order of its letters, such as SMET and MSTE, and finally settling as STEM in 2001. Over the past twenty-five years, STEM education has evolved from a clustering of four overlapping disciplines toward a more cohesive knowledge base and skill set. Recently, the scope has broadened to include the arts, and STEM is now sometimes called STEAM. The claim for this change in scope is that design thinking and creativity are essential for innovation.

The Work Pipelines

As the Cold War ended, the concern for national security diminished, and thus the American urgency to teach foreign languages included in the NDEA dropped. However, the need to prepare the technical workforce did not. Throughout the 1970s, 1980s, and 1990s, personal computers, cell phones, and technological innovations were developed. The presence of everyday technologies involving some form of computational power grew exponentially. By 2007, the report "Rising Above the Gathering Storm," published by the National Academies of Sciences, Engineering, and Medicine, warned that the United States was again falling behind in STEM abilities compared to other countries. By showing that STEM jobs are linked to prosperity and innovation, the report predicted dire consequences if the country could not compete in the global economy as the result of a poorly prepared workforce.

Although the report was disputed by some, it focused the federal conversation on STEM and led, in part, to the passing of the America Creating Opportunities to Meaningfully Promote Excellence in Technology, Education, and Science Act (or America COMPETES Act). At the same time, two international evaluations, the Trends in Mathematics and Science Study and the Programme for International Student Assessment showed that American students ranked poorly in math and science in comparison to their international counterparts.

In response, the government and nonprofit organizations decided again to fund and improve STEM education. This time the goal was to have an impact on workforce preparation—and ultimately economic competitiveness. Attention was placed on raising awareness about STEM careers, in particular with underrepresented groups (e.g., women and girls) and minorities. Efforts flourished to provide a deeper understanding of STEM content through interdisciplinary applications and problem-solving activities. Most of these early initiatives focused on overlapping disciplines such as math and science and left out computer science.

As the economy grew to need a technologically savvy workforce, the "T" in STEM started to shine. Today, STEM jobs in the United States continue to grow at a faster pace than employment in other occupational fields. STEM workers command higher wages than their non-STEM counterparts. With millions in funding for teacher training, curriculum development, and research grants, STEM education is now a household name that includes the discipline of computer science.

The tech boom of the 1990s and 2000s brought a modern-day Sputnik call, but this time it was focused on computer science. By 2011, a report by the National Research Council showed that computational thinking skills are essential in the K–12 curriculum for "succeeding in a technological society, increasing interest in the information technology professions, maintaining and enhancing U.S. economic competitiveness, supporting inquiry in other disciplines, and enabling personal empowerment." Furthermore, in the 2011 State of the Union Address, President Barack Obama stated, "This is our generation's Sputnik moment." It was his call for the United States to ramp up technological innovation to stay competitive, spur economic growth, and preserve national security.

In 2015, the STEM Education Act was passed. This was the first time that federal funding for STEM was extended to cover computer science programs. In addition, the National Science Foundation launched the STEM + C (Computer Partnerships) program for "helping all students—but particularly students in science, technology, engineering and mathematics disciplines—understand the role of computation and computational thinking within disciplinary problem solving" and "to build the evidence base for effective pedagogy and pedagogical environments that will make the integration of computing within STEM disciplines more age-appropriate and contemporaneously relevant to pre-K–12 STEM education." It is important to notice that attention was paid to beginning at an early age—in early childhood, elementary and secondary school, before stereotypes develop and pipelines are broken.

While computer science entered the federal agencies, well-funded nonprofits such as Code.org championed national and international awareness and access to computer science in schools, such as Computer Science Education Week and the popular Hour of Code. They launched curricular initiatives, new K–12 educational frameworks, professional development opportunities, and policy changes. Today, at the time of the writing of this book, Code.org has impacted over forty-two million students and one million teachers with all kinds of different programming in all fifty states.

A 2018 report by the Committee on STEM Education of the National Science and Technology Council shared a federal five-year strategic plan that highlights the importance of computer science for laying a strong foundation for the STEM workforce of the future: "Today's students are tomorrow's data analysts, artificial intelligence and machine learning specialists, software and applications developers, automation technicians, quantum information scientists, and cyber-security experts. For these reasons and more, a particularly strong area of emphasis within STEM education is computer science education."

The main propeller for the inclusion of computer science in education was the need to increase technical skills in the workplace. It was natural, then, to integrate it into the already existing umbrella of STEM. Although this chapter is focused on the United States as a case study, there is an increasing global trend to mandate the teaching of computer science in K–12 in multiple countries across all continents. Fortunately, there is still a healthy debate regarding the content to be taught, the pedagogies to use, and how to make it accessible and developmentally appropriate for all students.

Global Experience

At the time of writing this book, many countries are developing and implementing policies to bring computer science education to K–12 schools. Around the world, there are tensions regarding the best ways to integrate coding and computational thinking in the curriculum. While some countries teach it through specialized subjects such as computer science and robotics, others integrate them into already existing practices, thus linking computer science and computational thinking with content in other disciplines. Some countries promote the development of higher order skills, especially problem solving, while others prioritize the teaching of coding in a stand-alone format. It is too early yet to determine what approaches work best since we currently lack longitudinal data and large-scale comparative evaluations. In addition to making different pedagogical choices, countries differ in the timing they choose to initiate the teaching of computer science. Some start in the early grades, while others in high school to enhance job-related programs.

To the best of my knowledge, one of the first countries in the world to understand the potential of coding as a new way of thinking and expression was Costa Rica. Established in 1988, the Costa Rican Computers in Elementary Education Program seeks "to prepare a new generation of children and teachers for the challenges of the future," explains Clotilde Fonseca, founding director of the program and the Omar Dengo Foundation. Fonseca continues that "from the beginning, its main emphasis has been on the development of creativity, thinking skills and problem-solving abilities—long-term benefits that are expected to impact upon the country's socio-economic and technological development."

Costa Rica installed telecommunications infrastructure and provided support services to both rural and urban schools, giving priority to underprivileged populations. In addition, it benefited from a long-lasting collaboration with Papert and his team who brought LOGO and the constructionist pedagogy to the country. At the time, the Costa Rican program was unique and visionary. It broke away from the international standard by focusing on very young children first and by introducing coding and computational thinking rather than merely computer literacy instruction.

Almost ten years later, in the 90s, Papert's vision also gave birth to Project Lighthouse in Thailand, an ambitious attempt to use coding to highlight new paths to learning. Given the diversity of needs of the Thai people's rural and urban populations, the goal was to provide examples of powerful technology-rich learning environments in the digital age as opposed to a blueprint for education. David Cavallo, who was then my office mate at the MIT Media Lab, took a leading role in the project and orchestrated the needed conditions for multiple pilot projects, or lighthouses, across the country to illuminate possible paths. Most of them where outside the structure of existing schools. For example, back in 1998, I worked in rural villages teaching workshops on LOGO and LEGO robotics and helping teenagers learn HTML to create websites so that they could publish their own newspapers and explore the nascent field of e-commerce to sell their arts and crafts directly without the need of intermediaries.

Cavallo recounts how the project was first conceived in 1997, when "a group of Thai industrialists, educators, and government officials had come to believe that the considerable economic success Thailand had achieved in the previous decade could not be sustained unless the educational system could help develop learners who could function productively in a global, knowledge-based economy. They further believed that trying to incrementally reform the school system would take too long, cost too much, and still leave them, after perhaps twenty years of effort, with the same problems the rest of the developed world has now."

When I started my journey at the MIT Media Lab, I was lucky to experience firsthand how constructionism and the ideas that I describe in this book had an impact on teachers and children in both Thailand and Costa Rica. While I spent more time in Thailand and got to work directly with children, I traveled twice to Costa Rica, met with Clotilde Fonseca and Eleonora Badilla, and participated in several workshops. I noticed the impact that this long-lasting creative approach to coding had.

Years later, I visited Costa Rica again, this time to bring ScratchJr. While the Costa Rican case exemplifies an early experience of what a developing nation can accomplish given a sustained commitment to a vision, more recently other countries in Central and Latin America have been working to implement policies and programs to bring coding and computational thinking into their schools. Colombia, Uruguay, Chile, and Argentina are among those. I was fortunate to be involved in providing some of the training on both ScratchJr and KIBO for teachers in my home city of Buenos Aires. Throughout the book, different vignettes recount that work.

Across the ocean, in Europe, over forty-four countries are integrating coding into the curriculum at the national, regional, or local level, including Austria, Belgium, Bulgaria, the Czech Republic, Denmark, Estonia, Finland, France, Hungary, Ireland, Lithuania, Malta, Poland, Portugal, Slovakia, Spain, and the UK. In Asia, countries such as Singapore are embarking on an ambitious project to start as early as preschool. Steve Leonard, the executive deputy chairman of Singapore's Infocomm Media Development Authority who launched the initiative, understood that "as Singapore becomes a Smart Nation, our children will need to be comfortable creating with technology." Singapore is trying to change the idea of what technology in preschool settings looks like, from a screen-based approach to a maker-centered approach.

Singapore's vision is consistent with the coding playground. As a result of this, I was invited to participate in the nationwide Play-Maker Programme that, at the time, introduced robotics making and computational thinking to 160 preschool centers across Singapore. I trained a first cohort of early childhood teachers, conducted research with KIBO as part of the initiative, and experienced first-hand how the playfulness and learning in the coding playground was infused with the uniqueness of the palette of virtues of a diverse multicultural and multilingual society in Singapore.

Other countries such as Australia, Israel, Japan, New Zealand, Nigeria, South Africa, South Korea, Taiwan, and Turkey are also developing policies and programs to bring computer science and computational thinking to a wide population of students. This is not surprising since in an increasingly high-tech and connected world, digital devices and the internet are transforming society. Thus, computer science plays a major role in all domains, from shopping to voting.

Computer Science and Computational Thinking

Despite its current high visibility across the world, the value of incorporating computer science in K–12 education dates back to the 1960s. For example, in 1963, as president of the Association of Computing Machinery (ACM), computer scientist Alan Perlis observed that since computer programming requires logical and creative thought, its teaching needs to start early in life and become part of everyone's education. Perlis received the inaugural Turing Award in 1966 and was known as a founding father of computer science as a separate discipline. His insights echoed Papert's beliefs that learning programming empowers people to think in new ways.

In the early 2000s, distinguished computer scientist Jeannette Wing popularized the term *computational thinking* to refer to these "new ways of thinking." In a seminal 2006 article, she defined computational thinking as "solving problems, designing systems and understanding behaviors by drawing upon the concepts of Computer Science." More colloquially, computational thinking encompasses a set of processes that defines a problem, breaks it down into components, and develops models to solve the problem and then evaluates the result, iterates changes, and does it again.

Echoing Perlis and Papert, Wing argued that computational thinking is a problem-solving skill set that, although rooted in computer science, is universally applicable and therefore should be a part of every child's analytical ability. Wing's definition of computational thinking puts a heavy weight on solving problems algorithmically. In contrast, Papert's original concept involved the ability to think in new ways, not only as a means to solve problems but also for personal expression. A child who can think like a computer is a child who can use the computer to express herself in a fluent way. She is a child who masters another language, a language of logic and abstraction.

There is agreement that computational thinking requires a broad set of cognitive abilities, including, but not limited to, elements of abstraction, pattern recognition, conceptualization, sequencing, planning, and problem solving. However, researchers actively discuss whether computational thinking merits its own cognitive category or if it relies on other areas of thought. While the debate continues, the term made it into the school curriculum and educational policies. Today, most countries advocate for the teaching of computational thinking, and not only coding, to start in kindergarten.

Unfortunately, computers and other technological devices are still expensive. The unplugged movement proposes low-cost approaches to help people think like computer scientists without investing in expensive hardware and software that ultimately becomes obsolete every few years. Unplugged activities and games expose children to powerful ideas from computer science that can be introduced without a programming language. These place emphasis on promoting computational thinking rather than on learning the syntax of a particular coding language.

Unplugged computing grew appealing for the early childhood educational segment, not only because it is affordable but also because it promises to expose children to computational thinking while limiting screen time. For example, an unplugged computer science activity in kindergarten might involve directing a teacher who plays robot by giving her commands to reach an object in the room. Other examples include playing board games with decision trees, creating bead necklaces in binary with beads that represent ones and zeros, using a grid and symbols to put classic fairy tales in a logical order, and making a peanut butter sandwich following a set of instructions or algorithm.

Although unplugged activities can engage children in computational thinking, they do not expose them to programming or the ability to master a new artificial language. A child playing with a board game might problem-solve but might not understand the possibilities and challenges associated with learning a programming language and using it to make an expressive project. Languages, both natural and artificial, provide opportunities to create and inhabit new worlds and, ultimately, meaning-making. Children who are not exposed early on might be at a disadvantage. There is a risk of a growing new digital divide: those who can *think* computationally and those who can *act* computationally. And of course, there will be those who can do neither.

Children in wealthier neighborhoods may be exposed to coding through tablets, computers, and robots from an early age. They may learn programming languages to create the artifacts and systems they need, and they will develop their own voices and appropriate the tools. However, those from poorer neighborhoods might not be exposed and fall victim to the new illiteracy of the twenty-first century. In an increasingly technological and complex global economy, computational thinking and learning how to code need to come together. We need a new generation of innovators who know the languages to create a more fair and better world and not only think about it.

The Problem with STEM

As I described earlier in the chapter, in the United States the history of the consolidation of STEM, launched by the Sputnik I, originated in the need to maintain international primacy, a strong economy, and national security. Back in the late 50s, there was also a push for teaching foreign languages alongside math and science. However, after the end of the Cold War, with the emergence of a new world order and the growing industry of digital technologies, the foreign language component slowly disappeared and computer science became stronger in the STEM cluster.

However, things could have turned out differently. For example, what if instead of linking computer programming to economic growth and workforce preparation, it had also been linked to literacy? What if the early argument was that coding is the new literacy of the twenty-first century and therefore needs to be taught to everyone early on, alongside reading and writing? What if the pedagogies for teaching coding had also borrowed methods from literacy instruction instead of just math? Would this have prevented the current lack of women and underrepresented minorities in the field? Would the cluster of STEM disciplines still own computer science, and would computer science become another way to engage in critical thinking? Would computational thinking be incorporated into every subject? What if the role of computer science was conceived, from the beginning, as a tool to both educate the future workforce and educate the future citizenry? What can the field of computer science education learn from the rich history of textual literacy to support educational interventions for all? Might the invisible bridge between STEM and natural languages traced back to the 50s serve to create a gateway to new forms of teaching and learning and to new populations of learners?

Only a subset of the world's problems can be solved by STEM. Grouping computer science with STEM subjects restricts the power of coding to a limited group of disciplines, to a limited group of students and teachers, and to the particular demands of the workforce. It limits coding's power as a true literacy that promotes new ways of thinking and changing the world. As more people learn to code and computer programming leaves the exclusive domain of computer science and becomes central to other professions, the civic dimension of literacy comes into play. We are leaving the scribal age, when literacy was just for a few chosen ones. We are entering the printing press era, where the power of computation is for the masses.

A Window into Their World: Programming a Map, Building a Language

In Watertown, Massachusetts, the parents of the kindergarten class of a small Jewish day school gather for a special morning. The children will show the Hebrew skills they acquired during the year. The Jewish Community Day School (JCDS) is an immersive school in which children learn both English and Hebrew through the day. This is a big moment for everyone. As families walk into the school's multipurpose room, they see a huge map on the floor and a three-dimensional installation with a landscape that resembles the hills and deserts of Israel. As they get closer, they can see small orange robots stationed next to wooden blocks neatly arranged in sequences. Posters also hang on the walls with drawings and pictures done by the children.

As the event begins, a teacher welcomes the guests and explains that during Hebrew class, children learned a popular song called *"Eretz Yisrael Sheli"* ("My Land of Israel"), which tells the story of the different elements that were planted and built by the earlier pioneers: trees, roads, and bridges, all of which make the land beautiful. The teacher explains that "at JCDS we teach Hebrew and celebrate our connection to Israel as part of our heritage and religion. However, this time, the kindergarten students not only learned the Hebrew vocabulary of the song, but they also learned the KIBO robotics language." The room becomes noisy as some children clap. "We chose this song," continues the teacher, "because it has a clear sequence of events and repetition. That is very good for both vocabulary memorization and for thinking about a sequence of steps needed to be programmed in the KIBOs."

JCDS has an integrated curriculum, and teachers organize content from different disciplines into meaningful projects as much as possible. This time, they chose to bring together the learning of two different languages: KIBO robotics and Hebrew. As children studied the song's Hebrew vocabulary (house, trees, farm, etc.), they also programmed the KIBO robots to travel across the map in sync with the lyrics (figure 3.1).

The KIBOs were decorated with colorful paper and strings. One boasted a brilliant flame, symbolic of the passion for learning and curiosity that the school seeks to inspire in its students. Another displayed the Israeli and US flags riding on the backs of the KIBO to epitomize the immersive Hebrew/English experience the school provides. When students press a KIBO's "on" button, the robot flashes different colors of light as music fills the room. One KIBO dances away from the others, twirls, and comes back, signaling the others' turn to spin and shake to the music. Another one waits for

Figure 3.1
Map created by the children with a poster displaying KIBO's code.

a student to clap before starting its journey. All of the KIBOs move across the landscape and perform their unique routines.

When all KIBOs reach their destinations and stop their dances, children congregate and sing together *"Eretz Yisrael Sheli."* Friends and family clap profusely, and the room is full of energy and pride. After the formal presentation ends, guests are invited to engage with the young engineers. Every visitor is handed a sheet listing sample questions to initiate a conversation with the children. "How does your robot know where to go?" asks a grandmother. "I programmed it," responds Ronit, a jumping five-year-old. "But where is the computer?" continues grandma. Ronit replies, "You don't need a computer. KIBO is the computer. You just use these blocks to tell KIBO what to do. And then, you scan them. Like this." She proceeds to show how it works. "This is KIBO's language," explains Ronit. "Like I speak English and I am learning Hebrew, KIBO speaks these wooden blocks. Well, it doesn't really speak them, but it understands them. See, here?" Ronit points to the arrow and words in a blue motion block. "This block tells KIBO to move."

In this short exchange, Ronit clearly sees programming as a system of communication: "You tell KIBO what to do." Programming is a means to communicate with the robot. The agency is on the child, and she decides what she wants to communicate. However, like in any system of communication, there is always a minimum of two: a sender and a receiver. Ronit's explanation shows an awareness that KIBO needs to understand the language to do what it was commanded. This powerful idea applies not only to programming languages but also to natural languages used by humans.

Behind the final project was a tremendous amount of work and collaboration from both teachers and students. The children worked in teams of two or three. The teaching team was composed of a lead teacher who is Jewish and spoke minimal Hebrew, an Israeli teacher who was responsible for the Hebrew language immersion, and a non-Jewish STEM teacher. These three teachers coordinated the learning of key Hebrew vocabulary, the study of the song, the art project that built the map and landscape of Israel, and the programming skills to make KIBO travel around the map at the right tempo with the song's lyrics. Humor ensued as the kindergarten students had to constantly remind the STEM teacher what each refrain in the all-Hebrew song referred to. "Is this the house part?" she would ask with a smile. "No," they would respond in unison, "That word means farm!"

In this kindergarten integrated Hebrew/robotics unit, children learned about the design process, algorithms, repeat loops, and debugging. They also explored new vocabulary in a second language. They worked hard and had successes and frustrations. They learned how to solve problems, integrated the arts through their drawings of the landscape, worked together, honed their Hebrew vocabulary, and used math to count how many KIBO steps it

would take to move from point A to B. Furthermore, they confidently stepped into the role of experts, sharing all they had learned
throughout the curriculum during the final exhibit. It was a celebration of their accomplishments, even if some of the KIBOs ran
out of batteries or steered away from their original path on the map.
It did not matter. The accomplishment was not a polished performance but instead the learning process.

4

Coding as Another Language

Annie (five years old): My robot comes from Egypt.
Lara (five years old): How do you know?
Annie: It reads hieroglyphics.
Lara: Mine reads price tags, like in the supermarket.
Annie: Yes, that is hieroglyphics.

In August 1994, I moved to Boston from Buenos Aires to attend graduate school. With the move, I left behind not only my family and my city but also my native language. I love Spanish; I can truly express myself in it. For example, I started to keep a diary when I was twelve years old, and in high school, I received an award for one of my stories. In college, my friend Florencia Arbiser and I taught an after-school writing workshop for children. I did coursework in journalism, and because writing came easily for me, I was offered a full-time job while still in school. I spent my undergraduate education working as a junior editor at a popular magazine in the mornings and attending university to study "social communication sciences" in the afternoons. I woke up every morning with written words in Spanish and did not stop using them until bedtime.

The move to Boston meant, among many changes, losing my confidence and my expertise with the mainstream written language. With effort, I slowly learned to replace the long, twisted Spanish narrative for the direct, to-the-point English. During the first few years, I missed Spanish; I missed the metaphors, the sentence constructions, and the word etymologies. English was a new challenge. While I became comfortable using it in academia, I did not enjoy reading novels or poems in English. I also kept my diary in Spanish. Slowly, I embarked on the long journey of finding pleasure in the written language of my new home. Knowing the syntax and the grammar of a written language is not the same as comfortably expressing ourselves with it: our dreams and fears, our hidden memories and hopeful futures, our passions and dreads. It takes time to grow a language. For me, it only happened once I felt comfortable with the American culture. Language and culture come hand in hand.

Over the last two-and-a-half decades, my work with children has focused on creating programming languages and innovative cultures of learning. In 1997, I developed SAGE (Storytelling Agent Generation Environment) for my master's thesis at the MIT Media Lab under the supervision of Justine Cassell. This authoring tool engaged children in programming wise storytellers to interact with.

SAGE was inspired by Eliza, created by Joseph Weizenbaum in the early '70s. While doing research on artificial intelligence and natural language understanding, Weizenbaum made a simple computer program that simulates a psychotherapist called Eliza. Eliza mirrors what the client says; it is a "dumb" program that only recognizes character strings, responds by making grammatical substitutions, and does not understand meaning. Although Eliza's first users were technically sophisticated, Weizenbaum's students, and colleagues who knew the limitations of the program, they still engaged with it in a deep and personal way.

Something similar happened with SAGE. Children programmed their own wise storytellers to engage in personal conversations. In return, SAGE would offer an inspirational story. Children were both programmers and users. SAGE's simple graphical editor allowed children to program the flow of the conversational interaction and to create a database of comforting stories. They annotated each of the stories with keywords so that they could be matched by the system. As the conversation progressed between the SAGE character and the user, stories were triggered when keywords were matched. For example, if the user was writing about her mother, the SAGE matching system would find an inspirational story in the database that contained the word mother or a synonym.

In addition, to make SAGE more appealing for young children and to explore tangible interfaces at a time in which these were novel, I created a robotic bunny with hidden servomechanisms that could also be programmed by the children. The bunny's role was to be the SAGE storyteller's assistant. Children could program the movements of the stuffed animal. For example, if the bunny was "listening" to the user's problems, it inclined its ears forward and blinked its eyes to indicate attentiveness (figure 4.1).

While programming SAGE was fun, it was even better to interact with it. During my research, both children and adults created wise storytellers from different traditions. My favorites were a Hasidic rabbi and a Buddhist scholar. When interacting with them, children revealed aspects of their inner lives and the problems they faced every day. Following research guidelines to protect children's privacy and safety, logs were kept and analyzed. The following is a sample resulting from a conversation log between Leo, a thirteen-year-old, and a character programed to behave like a Hasidic rabbi:

SAGE: You seem a little shy, Leo. I also was shy to tell stories, but since my father and my grandfather were Hasidic rabbis I knew I had to become one. That is the way it is. Leo how old are you?

USER: 13

SAGE: Oy vey, I am 77 years older than you. You know Leo, a story is more than a story . . . a story has power. What is your story?

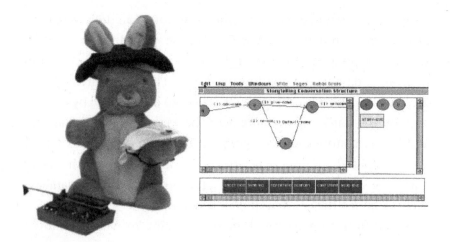

Figure 4.1
The SAGE system with a programmable stuffed rabbit, storyteller's assistant, and programming interface

USER: I had my first day at school today and everybody was making fun of me because I did not know the text.

SAGE: Oy vey . . . go on, Leo.

USER: So they started to beat me up because I was so stupid.

SAGE: I understand—what more can you tell me Leo?

USER: And every day when I come home from school I cry for a long time.

SAGE: Do you think you are the first one in this situation? Leo, let me tell you a story: When Rabbi Wolf Zbarazer was on a journey, he would not permit the driver to beat his horses, saying to him: "You have no need even to scold them, if you understand how to address them properly." Can you find a connection with your own story?

In this example, the child, Leo, shares his problems at school with the Hasidic SAGE who tells him an inspirational story from the database by matching nouns, verbs, and values. In the next sample, the same format is used, but this time the interaction happens between a Taoist SAGE who tells a comforting story to another boy named Conor, who is also experiencing problems with school:

SAGE: Ni hau. What is your name?

USER: Conor.

SAGE: My name is Chuang-Tzu. I am a Taoist master who lives by the Way, the Tao, wandering free and easy. How old are you, Conor?

USER: 13.

SAGE: I am 87 years older than you. I am older than the mountains and the seas, while you, Conor are still young. You are here because you seek knowledge. Conor, tell me your troubles, and I will enlighten you with the sayings of the Tao, the Way.

USER: I want to do better in school. I have a lot of math homework, and I don't understand all of it.

SAGE: Go on, Conor. We are becoming one.

USER: The teacher was vague in explaining it.

SAGE: I see, Conor. Maybe this teaching of the Way will help you. To understand others is to be knowledgeable; to understand yourself is to be wise. To conquer others is to have strength; to conquer yourself is to be strong. To know when you have enough is to be rich. To go forward with strength is to have ambition. To not lose your place is to last long. To die but not be forgotten, that's true long life. Do you get it?

USER: Yes, I'm supposed to learn from my mistakes.

SAGE: So, Conor, now you understand the Way. I must go now to become one again with heaven and earth. Conor, don't stop thinking about the Way, and you will find your own way. May you, Conor, become one with the Tao.

Over sixty young children engaged with the Hasidic and the Taoist sages. They both told their own stories and interpreted the hidden meaning behind the inspirational stories offered by the sages. As my research progressed, I worked with many young people who were able to suspend disbelief and engage in the storytelling interactions with different characters.

Over the two-year period of my master's thesis, I used SAGE in different classrooms, hospital settings, and after-school environments. In creating a SAGE, children designed that person to whom they wished they could turn to with their problems. They also played with different notions of self by creating or imitating the narrative voices they wanted or needed to hear. Children programmed storytellers as projections of fears, feelings, interests, and role models. For example, while some chose to create characters such as Mother Nature, Shaquille O'Neil, and the Big Orange Fox, young cardiac patients used SAGE to create Mrs. Needle or Mr. Tape as a way of coping with cardiac illness, hospitalizations, and invasive medical procedures.

Over time, I refined the authoring environment and created experiments to adjust the matching system between users' personal stories and inspirational stories in the database. I learned that when the matching system was off, meaning the computer could not make any match, it did not matter. Children still interpreted the offered inspirational stories according to their own situations. There was no matching algorithm needed. Children created sports stars, grandmothers, doctors, cartoon characters, and historical figures. They interacted with them and shared them with others. In the process, they explored the power of both natural and artificial languages. As an augmented Eliza, SAGE offered a limited programming language. However, as a tool for expression, it had unlimited possibilities.

A few years later, for my doctoral work under the mentorship of Seymour Papert, I extended SAGE into a virtual world called Zora. At the time, three-dimensional virtual spaces were not popular, as the field was just beginning. In Zora, users were graphically represented as avatars, which could both navigate and build a virtual city. They had tools to create 3D objects and to program conversational interactions for each of these objects (figure 4.2). While constructing the city's private and public spaces children could also converse with other children in real time through a graphical chat system.

Figure 4.2
Zora City Hall

In Zora, all virtual objects had three different kinds of attributes that needed to be personalized by the children: the *presentation attributes* determined the object's graphical appearance and motion, the *administration attributes* determined who owns the object and can therefore edit it, and the *narrative attributes* determined the object's conversational flow and stories as well as the personal and ethical values that were used to tag it. For example, a flower could be tagged with the value "love of nature" by one child and "responsibility for nature" by a different child. While presentation and administration attributes are needed for any graphical virtual world, the narrative ones were unique to Zora. They provided a structure for thinking about the role of objects as carriers of both ideas about self and community and personal and moral values. In addition, they served to launch conversations between children about the different values used to tag similar objects and the universality of some of them.

The following vignette describes a Zora experience during a summer workshop for teens to explore cultural and religious differences.

Sixteen-year-old Janet connects to Zora, a multiuser virtual city. There, during a summer workshop for youth, she has created an avatar, a virtual representation of herself, a virtual home, and a Jewish temple. A visit to Janet's virtual home on Zora reveals much about her: her favorite friends, her most-loved games, and her family's history. After working on her own virtual home, she creates the Jewish temple. She makes a virtual rabbi to welcome visitors with a blessing.

She invites other children to make the decorations of the virtual synagogue. There are Hebrew letters, a map of Israel, and a picture of a man praying. Janet clicks on a silver mezuzah (a small piece of parchment inscribed with biblical passages from Deuteronomy, which is rolled up in a container and affixed by many Jewish households to their door frames in conformity with Jewish law and as a sign of their faith). It tells her a story about the meaning of the prayers it holds.

She decides to add a television to the temple. Inside it, she puts a snapshot from the movie *Schindler's List* that she found on the web. The system enables her to associate objects with values. She associates the television with the value "documentation" and defines it as "very important to remember history. That way, bad things won't happen again. Holocaust survivors are getting very old now, and if someone doesn't record their stories of what happened, we are doomed to forget and repeat the horrors." While exploring the Jewish temple, Janet encounters Marie. Both girls chat via their avatars, and then Marie invites Janet to visit the virtual Baptist church she created.

Although Zora had colorful graphics and playful ways to construct and navigate the virtual world, it was the stories and the conversations that pulled children to it. The community was more appealing than the coding. We learned all of this by looking at the Zora system logs. Zora provided tools for researchers and teachers to evaluate the experience by keeping a log, with dates and times, of everything users said or did online. At the time, this was innovative.

For my doctoral thesis, I worked with Zora with different populations of preteens and teens who created their own virtual worlds and narrative interactions. Middle schoolers participated in a virtual Zora summer camp to explore diversity issues. Pediatric patients with renal disease shared coping strategies while facing hemodialysis. Later on, after graduating from MIT and starting as an assistant professor at Tufts University, through generous funding from the CAREER program at the National Science Foundation, I was able to continue working with Zora. This time, my focus was children who received organ transplants and had long hospitalizations and with teenagers all over the world who created a virtual clubhouse to learn about each other's cultures and countries. I also did work with incoming freshman at Tufts who created a virtual campus to express their feelings about starting college life.

Back in early 2000, when I did all of this work, Zora and three-dimensional virtual worlds were novel technologies. However, the idea of using the power of computation to help children express themselves dates back to the late 1960s when Seymour Papert and colleagues developed LOGO. In my own trajectory as a researcher, my work is about finding ways to use technology for identity expression and for exploration of values. Who we are is connected to the values we hold and cherish. Thus, I always try to work with both. In my early projects, SAGE and Zora, I also highlighted the relationships between natural and artificial languages in a more salient way than with ScratchJr or KIBO. Back then, my target population was preteens and teens, a time when alphabetical literacy has already developed, and it was possible to engage in more sophisticated explorations.

My focus has now shifted age groups. I mostly work with younger children who have not yet mastered written language. However, my mission remains the same: providing opportunities for children to express themselves and their values through using technologically rich socially situated symbolic systems of representation. With their own grammar and syntax, these artificial languages can be used to convey meaning, to create something new, to communicate things that are displaced in time or space, and to build community. There is magic power in written languages, both natural and artificial. Think about it: the Spanish alphabet has twenty-seven letters, English has twenty-six, ScratchJr has twenty-eight blocks, and KIBO has twenty-one. However, there is an almost infinite number of ways to express ourselves with these limited numbers.

Transitioning Languages

Coding is a new literacy. For something to be deemed as a literacy "means that it is important to the status and financial health of a nation," writes Annette Vee in her 2017 book, *Coding Literacy: How Computer Programming Is Changing Writing*. Coding is perceived as involving a set of skills and knowledge that today's society highly values. It serves to build a competitive workforce in the global economy and is infrastructural for daily life across many different sectors. Other domains have also attained the literacy status: health literacy, cultural literacy, visual literacy, and so forth. However, the achievement of alphabetical literacy was a world-changing event. This kind of literacy is both instrumental and epistemological. It enables us to do new things and to organize social practices around symbol systems but also restructures the way we know the world and the way we think.

Walter Ong, an American Jesuit priest and scholar, documented a fundamental shift in the form of thought while studying societies that are transitioning from orality to literacy. Ong wrote that "without writing, the literate mind would not and could not think as it does, not only when engaged in writing but even when it is composing its thoughts in oral form. [. . .] The fact that we do not commonly feel the influence of writing on our thoughts shows that we have interiorized the technology of writing so deeply that without tremendous effort we cannot separate it from ourselves or even recognize its presence and influence."

Ong describes writing as a technology that must be learned. After mastery, there is a transformation of thinking from the world of sound to the world of sight. For example, oral cultures might not understand the concept of "looking something up." It would have no meaning because without writing, words have no visual presence, even when the objects they represent are visual. Spoken words happen in time, not in space. Words are sounds and visual metaphors cannot describe them.

Oral cultures use mnemotechnic strategies for preserving information over time in the absence of writing. For example, some rely on proverbs, condensed wisdom, epic poetry, and characters. These oral cultures favor cyclic thought. The shaman or storyteller invites people to hear stories, which are told in iterative, redundant ways to aid with memory. In contrast, cultures of literacy favor linear, logical, historical, or evolutionary thought, which depend on writing.

Literacy is an historical and social phenomenon with strong epistemological implications. The technologies of writing, which have changed over time, have impacted the world of knowledge. The printing press facilitated the wide distribution of ideas, while the early scribes kept knowledge isolated for just a few chosen people. Due to his interest in cultures transitioning from orality to literacy, Ong noticed how early criticism of computers had similarities to early criticism of literacy. Both blamed the new technology (writing or coding) for the potential loss of memory and intellectual capability.

This is nothing new. Centuries earlier, Plato had already criticized writing. Despite this, earlier critiques might have missed the fundamental ways in which both writing and coding restructure our thinking. They support logical sequential thinking and allow the separation of the subject from the produced object. The resulting production takes a life of its own and can be analyzed, deconstructed, fixed, and interpreted.

This process is likely to trigger metacognition: "thinking about thinking." Papert used to say that "you can't think about thinking without thinking about thinking about something." In his witty way, he was referring to the importance of understanding our own way of knowing and making sense of the world. In his view, the computer, and the ability to program it, provided an opportunity for children to create a "something" (i.e., a computational project) for thinking about thinking.

Meaningful Sequences

In a first-grade classroom, Ms. Lorna begins to introduce students to robotics. The students eagerly situate themselves at their tables and hush as she starts reciting the children's book *There Was an Old Lady Who Swallowed a Fly*. While reading, Ms. Lorna points to various uses of repetition, a term the students have recently learned in English class. She calls upon them to raise their hands when repetition is used throughout the story. Again and again, students' hands shoot up across the classroom at the countless repeating words or phrases. Ms. Lorna refers to the predictability of this repetition as a pattern. At the end of the story, Ms. Lorna explains that repetition is not only essential in natural languages such as English but also in programming languages such as KIBO.

Soon after, she takes out the KIBO robot, and the children become happy and clap. In the front of the room, holding KIBO high so that everyone can see, she asks for a volunteer to help her hold the KIBO blocks. Ms. Lorna starts to make a program using a begin block followed by four forward blocks. Intentionally, she leaves out the end block that is necessary to complete the program. Without hesitation, the class shouts all together: "You forgot the end block!" Ms. Lorna reacts with surprise, all the while aware of the mistake, and says, "Thank you for debugging my program!" She then asks, "What is repeating in my now complete program?" An eager student shoots his hand into the air and answers, "The forward block!" Ms. Lorna nods approvingly and follows with a second question: "How many times does it repeat, class?" Students respond by lifting their four fingers high. Ms. Lorna nods in affirmation and explains, "We have now created a repeating pattern of blocks, just as we read a story with repeating patterns of words." Then she adds with enthusiasm, "Now let's run the program!"

Another student volunteers to do the routine scanning program with KIBO. Signaling a successful job, KIBO alerts the student that it is ready to run its program with a flashing green button. As the student presses play, KIBO begins to move forward four steps until completing its program. Variations of chants for KIBO fill the room while the robot moves, followed by a large sigh as KIBO comes to a stop. A student shouts out, "I want KIBO to go forward for even longer!" Ms. Lorna animatedly responds, "How do you suggest we do that, Aaliyah?"

Aaliyah takes a moment to think before responding. "Maybe if we use more forward blocks, like one hundred of them!" Ms. Lorna seizes the moment to go back to the concept of repetition and teach a new KIBO block and says, "That's a great idea, Aaliyah! Unfortunately, we do not have one hundred forward blocks—but there is another way."

The students pay attention as the teacher goes back into KIBO's kit to pull out two new blocks. "This is what we call a repeat loop," the teacher says and shows the gray begin block and the end repeat block. "We use these blocks when we want KIBO to repeat an action, like going forward." Ms. Lorna puts the forward block in-between the loop created by the gray begin block and the end repeat block and says, "See! It is like we are making a cheese sandwich. The forward block is our cheese, and it goes in-between the two slices of the bread, the beginning and the end repeat blocks."

"But how do we tell KIBO how many times to repeat going forward?" inquires a student. Ms. Lorna explains to them the use of parameters, a numbered or infinite small card that attaches to the repeat block with Velcro. "I do not see a one hundred card," says Aaliyah, but she adds, "Let's make it repeat infinite times, forever. That is better than one hundred." The other children agree and start giggling. Ms. Lorna creates a new program using the repeat loop, forward block, and the infinite parameter card. After KIBO is scanned and begins its run, Aaliyah makes an observation: "This is great. It would have taken a really long time to scan one hundred blocks. And this is like a one hundred. It's even a lot more, nonstop!" Ms. Lorna responds by affirming to the class, "Exactly, repeat loops make it easier to scan a KIBO program that has a repeating pattern!"

The class is now eager to program on their own. The teacher tells the students to get into their KIBO playgroups to begin assembling their own repeat loop programs. The room bustles as students work in their small groups to create repeating patterns of various kinds: motion, sound, and light blocks. As students finish building their programs, they work together in roles such as scanner and assistant to scan their programs. While some groups build their repeating patterns, others struggle to have KIBO run a program. Frustration is evoked in the echoes of foot-stomping and loud sighs. However, students know that debugging is part of the coding process, and they get at it. Elated groups with elaborate programs beckon Ms. Lorna to watch their KIBO repeat their programs several, if not infinite, times. As the lesson ends, students begin to clean up. The students assigned to the group organizer role take charge, placing each KIBO part back into its respective bin, as they have done many times.

Ms. Lorna's classroom was following the CAL KIBO curriculum developed by my DevTech Research Group at Tufts University. This curriculum introduces powerful ideas of computer science, such as repeat loops, in direct conversation with powerful ideas from literacy, such as repetition. However, before getting to this, it focuses on the concept of sequencing. Sequences can be found in natural languages through words and stories and also in artificial languages; algorithms are sequences of instructions for a robot or program to follow.

At its simplest level, computer programming is the activity of putting together a sequence of instructions. In the process of making this sequence, the programmer engages in abstract, logical thinking. Although most of us can identify the act of thinking and recognize its value, there is no scholarly consensus on its definition. Thinking is the ability to represent, model, make sense, interpret, predict, and invent our experiences in the world. Thinking is facilitated by language. As Soviet psychologist Lev Vygotsky wrote, "Thought development is determined by language, i.e., by the linguistic tools of thought." Thus, as educators, we strive to help children develop one of the most powerful tools for thinking: natural written languages. In the coding playground, we give them another tool: artificial programming languages.

Early childhood education has many strategies for building language skills and supporting the transition from oral to written language. The teaching of literacy has occupied the early grades for a long time. Today, we have a new opportunity: teaching children how to think by using both natural and artificial languages. While humans understand written alphabets, smart objects only understand programming languages.

I am using the term *language*, whether natural or artificial, to refer to a formal representational system of signs, governed by syntactic and grammatical combinatory rules, that serves to communicate. This broad definition encompasses natural languages such as English, Spanish, Japanese, computer languages such as C or ScratchJr, sign languages, the musical notation system, and tangible languages such as KIBO robotics among others. Natural and artificial languages have a limited set of signs that represent meaning and can be combined in multiple ways following a set of rules. Research has explored the similarities and differences between natural and artificial languages, and interdisciplinary endeavors such as natural language processing and computational linguistics have emerged. Exploring those is beyond the scope of this book.

Here, I am sharing a pedagogical approach to make coding a literacy of the twenty-first century. The goal of literacy is to master the syntax and grammar but also the meanings and uses of the systems of representation. A literate person knows that reading and writing are tools for interpretation and, in time, tools of power. They support new ways of thinking. Echoing Brazilian educator Paulo Freire, literacy is a tool for critical comprehension, for understanding the world, and for actively changing it. He wrote in the early 70s and 80s that the written word is a tool for personal transformation and social change. His work inspired mass literacy campaigns as a way to liberate the oppressed. I believe this could be the same with coding. Furthermore, thinking of coding as a literacy give us access to new ways to teach both programming and reading and writing both literacies of the twenty-first century.

Philosophers like Ludwig Wittgenstein argued that the language we speak determines the thoughts we are able to have. Will using a logical programming language engage children in thinking in analytical ways? In other words, will learning a new language help form new patterns of thought, new conceptual frameworks, and new ways of using language?

I coined the term Coding as Another Language (CAL) to refer to a pedagogical approach for learning how to use a new language, a programming language. CAL proposes that programming, as a literacy, engages new ways of thinking and new ways of communicating and expressing ideas, not only new ways of problem solving. Languages are grounded in cultures. CAL promotes a learning culture in which I–Thou relationships can flourish in the process of learning to program; a learning culture in which the ten values of the palette of virtues are explored and practice; a learning culture that adds new virtues to the palette, adapts existing ones, and dives into what it means for each particular community to help children develop character strengths to make the world a better place. Coding is a semiotic act, a meaning-making activity.

Within the CAL pedagogy, learning to program is akin to learning how to use a written language, a socially situated system of symbolic representation. How do we learn languages? Extensive work has been done to understand the cognitive and neural basis that support the acquisition and use of natural languages, both in oral and written forms. However, few studies focus on artificial languages. This is not only an intellectual challenge but also a prerequisite for developing robust educational coding initiatives for children. If computer programming is a cognitive invention, like reading and writing, how do emergent skills, such as learning a new programming language, get incorporated into already existing ones? What are the mechanisms that facilitate this process? While there is a rich tradition of cognitive scientists, experimental and developmental psychologists, and psycholinguists doing basic research on how the brain learns to read and write, we need more research on the cognitive mechanisms involved when learning to code.

Some work explores the differences between expert and novice programmers and employs qualitative and quantitative methods to collect and analyze sample programs, surveys, and interview data. Other studies use tools such as fMRI (functional magnetic resonance imaging) to directly measure the blood flow in the brain, thereby providing information on brain activity. In our pilot work with a team of cognitive neuroscientists at MIT, we started to explore some of these questions by conducting exploratory studies using fMRI to capture what happens in the brain when people are coding. Although we do not have certainties, we learned that some aspects of the language system might be involved when doing certain tasks. We need more interdisciplinary teams working on these issues.

It took many decades and financial commitment for cognitive scientists and neuroscientists to grow a research agenda to explore the mechanisms involved in reading. What if the research agenda would extend to also explore what happens when learning to code? Are some of the cognitive mechanisms associated with coding also found with reading and writing? What pedagogical strategies could we put in place once we understand similarities and differences? As coding gains literacy status and is taught in schools, why wait to realize that many children are left behind? Would that influence our curricular grouping choices? Would we think of a different way to integrate coding rather than mostly with STEM disciplines?

This book proposes an alternative pathway. At a time when the United States, among other nations, is struggling to understand if, how, and when the teaching of computer science becomes mandatory, it is important to grapple with these questions before policies are put in place.

Doing Things with Language

A strong body of research has shown the mechanisms and social practices by which young children learn the alphabetical system of representation and what instructional strategies are most successful for teaching reading and writing. When successful, literacy instruction goes beyond coding and decoding by providing a tool for interpretation and expression. Furthermore, as Vee wrote, "A democracy—at least ideally—demands an informed citizenry, and when information circulates in texts, being informed means being able to read."

What happens when information is hidden in algorithms? Should everyone learn to program? How do we teach it? The CAL pedagogy is grounded in the principle that programming involves learning how to use a new symbolic system of representation for communicative and expressive functions. Therefore, decades of teaching children alphabetical literacy might offer insights. Research has shown how children transition from oral to written language through a series of fairly predictable stages culminating in the deep understanding, interpretation, and production of text.

Literacy instruction starts with spoken language. Given the right conditions, a child might unfold the ability to read and write, but she needs appropriate instruction. In teaching how to code, there is a myriad of unplugged games and e-toys that also leverage the use of spoken language to engage in computational thinking as a stepping-stone to further learning. It does not happen naturally; it requires teaching strategies. While some children might learn to code on their own, they usually follow a tutorial or find someone who can mentor them through their first steps. They master the language once they can express themselves with it.

Mitchel Resnick and David Siegel, when discussing the creation of the Scratch Foundation to promote an expressive approach to coding, wrote that "for us, coding is not a set of technical skills but a new type of literacy and personal expression, valuable for everyone, much like learning to write." Learning to program is more than job preparation. It is about using programming languages to express our ideas in systematic ways, to communicate and engage in creative problem solving, and to develop an informed citizenry who can change the world.

From smart watches to cell phones to automated cars, most of our daily objects have been programmed. Algorithms dictate the news displayed in our social media, the people we want to meet, and the merchandise we need to purchase. If we do not understand algorithms, we might not understand why and how certain information is or is not presented to us. Programming is a form of literacy; however, it has been taught as a special skill. Unfortunately, this approach has diminished coding's true power as a literacy that promotes new ways of thinking, new ways of acting in the world, and new ways of building communities.

The exclusivity of programming is reminiscent of reading and writing when it was taught only to scribes and monks at one point in history. At that time, books were expensive and safely kept by a minority who could afford them. Today, everyone needs to know how to read and write, and books are common in most households. Of course, neither literacy or coding are truly democratized, and inequities still exist between the rich and the poor. However, despite of this, according to the Global Age-Specific Literacy Projections Model produced by the UNESCO (United Nations Educational, Scientific and Cultural Organization) Institute for Statistics, the global literacy rate for all people aged fifteen and above is 86.3 percent. To the best of my knowledge, there are no large studies yet about people's coding literacy. However, a growing number of studies, such as those produced by the Pew Research Center, have documented the growth in the adoption and distribution of the internet, home technologies, and smartphones.

We do not teach people to write because they are going to be professional writers, and we should not teach them how to code so that they become software developers. If coding is a literacy for the twenty-first century, can it borrow strategies from alphabetic literacy to teach computer science? Can these strategies tap into children's character strengths and universal values to build caring communities in which I–Thou relationships are nurtured? Can those values be practiced and adapted based on local sociocultural contexts? That is the proposition behind the CAL approach.

A Window into Their World: Georgia, Elena, and the Old Lady

Georgia declares, "We need to deliver the frog!" While it was not entirely clear what Georgia means by this, it is obvious she has a plan for designing a KIBO program aligned with the story read by Ms. Stacey. She quickly begins to put blocks together. Georgia programs KIBO to spin forever "like a frog" and explains that she needs to "deliver the frog to the river" and "the frog spins because she is excited!" Georgia scans the programming blocks, and the KIBO frog moves forward until it reaches the river made of green construction paper. Once there, it spins round and round. "The frog is spinning now, but she doesn't know that she will be eaten by a cat," explains Georgia to Ms. Stacey, who asked about the connection between this project and the book they read in class, *There Was an Old Lady Who Swallowed a Fly.*

Ms. Stacey had read this story to her first-grade students, and together, as a group, they explored the sequence in which the old lady swallows increasingly large animals. After making sure they all got the right order of events, she invited them to retell the story of the old lady with their KIBOs but this time choosing the animals they would like the lady to swallow. The trick was that children needed to develop a logic for swallowing. For example, big animals can only swallow small animals. Children had to choose at least four animals for their sequence before the lady was able to swallow the last one that would cause her death.

Georgia explains that after the frog and the cat comes the eagle who will eat the cat and then the bear who will eat the eagle. "My old lady will not die when she eats the bear because she will vomit it back," explains Georgia. "Look!" and she shows Ms. Stacey how a KIBO with a black box and two eyes on top shakes three times. "That is my bear after the lady vomited him," smiles a proud, creative Georgia.

In a different corner of the classroom, Elena is showing Michaela her project. "I programmed KIBO to move forward and stop every time there is an animal on the floor." Elena's KIBO is dressed up with colorful cloth and represents the old lady. KIBO is programmed to beep every time it eats a new animal and to "move back and forth to show it is swallowing." Elena chose a different way to retell the story through KIBO. While in Georgia's story KIBO was dressed up as different animals and the old lady was not represented, in Elena's story KIBO was the old lady and the animals were plastic toys found in the classroom. Ms. Stacey is happy about the diversity of ways to tell and retell the story. She is also excited to see how her students were able to use multiple strategies in their coding and decorations (figure 4.3).

After informally visiting with each group, Ms. Stacey asked the class to come sit at the rug and bring their programming blocks and their KIBOs as well as anything else they would need to share their projects. During the technology circle, one by one of the ten children in this small class shared their robotic stories. Together they

Figure 4.3
Different versions of *There Was an Old Lady Who Swallowed a Fly*

laughed about the creative retelling and also identified sequences that did not have a clear logic.

All of this learning happened during a time identified by Ms. Stacey's school as "literacy block." However, Ms. Stacey was able to integrate the coding playground into the literacy block to address and strengthen one of the educational targets in the frameworks: the ability to tell and retell a story and the use of sequencing.

5

From Theory to Practice

Lila (six years old): Banana will get into the bus now and disappear. Watch!

Jenny (seven years old): It is still there. The bus is gone. It doesn't work.

Lila: I will fix it.

Jenny: Can you do it now?

Lila changes the location of the ScratchJr "hide" block in her sequence. She shows the program again to Jenny.

Jenny: That was fast! Can you fix my story? [She gives Lila a written paper.] I did not program it yet. But Mrs. Peterson says there are mistakes.

Lila: That will take longer for me because I have to read it first.

Over the years, I have learned that one of my favorite parts of doing research is working with teachers. By now, I have taught over a hundred professional development workshops, trainings, and special courses. Regardless of the location, Portugal, Singapore, Spain, Costa Rica, or Thailand, there is always an "aha" moment followed by laughter and a hug. That is the time when teachers truly get it.

At that time, teachers make an emotional connection to coding as another language, as a tool for expression. They realize they can create their own projects. They are proud to share with each other and take videos to show their students and often their own children and families. At that time, they connect with the values in the palette of virtues and understand that their determination, persistence, and patience were worth it. They are grateful to the group for providing help and support during the hard process of learning to code. They are honest with themselves and choose to keep working at problem solving because the project is not exactly what they hoped for. They also forgive themselves for being slow and for not getting it. At that moment, in every professional development workshop, teachers become confident that they will ultimately get their project to work.

While many teachers who participate in the trainings choose to come, others are sent by their principals or districts. Often, they are not interested in coding, and the reasons vary. Sometimes they want their young students to first master the three "Rs," the basic skills taught in schools: reading, writing, and arithmetic. Other times they believe that what is more important than teaching coding is to facilitate socioemotional learning: managing emotions, setting and achieving goals, developing empathy for others, establishing and maintaining positive relationships, and making responsible decisions. Usually they are just overwhelmed by their so many teaching responsibilities. As the training progresses and teachers understand that coding can provide opportunities for reinforcing academic skills, engaging in socioemotional learning and developing, and practicing character strengths and values, they relax, see the benefit, and start to enjoy the coding playground.

In some of my early writing, I used the acronym CAL for the phrase Coding as Literacy instead of Coding as Another Language. Research is never a neat straight line path. Ideas are messy, and it takes time. It takes sharing with others, hearing feedback, and engaging in discussions to further develop them. While the concept of Coding as Literacy has been advanced by many as an intellectual effort, I find that CAL has an interventionist tone to it. It is about how we teach coding and not only what coding is.

The CAL pedagogy positions the teaching and learning of programming as the study of a socially situated symbolic system of representation with communicative and expressive functions to promote I–Thou encounters. It is a pathway for character development, for exploring the socioemotional and ethical dimensions of learning, and for practicing values and building bridges through learning a new language. Ultimately, it helps us to understand that our actions, like the actions of anyone who creates, have consequences.

To make this pedagogy accessible, my DevTech Research Group at Tufts University developed the free CAL curriculum for both KIBO and ScratchJr. Designed for prekindergarten to second grade, it provides a scope and sequence for content and skills to be taught in a coding playground as well as opportunities to develop a palette of virtues by engaging in positive behaviors. While exploring the parallels between artificial and natural languages, CAL targets the whole child. It is grounded in the PTD theoretical framework, which I developed, and is inspired by the field of positive youth development and many conversations with my colleague Richard Lerner. In 2012 I described PTD extensively in my book *Designing Digital Experiences for Positive Youth Development: From Playpen to Playground.*

CAL offers coding activities and games involving cognitive and socioemotional aspects that engage children in six positive behaviors described by PTD: content creation, creativity, communication, collaboration, community building, and choices of conduct. These six behaviors, which we can often see at the neighborhod playground, can also be promoted in the coding playground. However, a coding playground needs guiding values, not only behaviors. The ten values in the palette of virtues intentionally serve this purpose: curiosity, open-mindedness, perseverance, patience, optimism, honesty, fairness, generosity, gratitude, and forgiveness.

New values can be added to the palette, and different blends can be mixed and matched according to the particular classroom and cultural context. For instance, while some teachers might focus on turn-taking, taking care of materials, and learning how to work collaboratively with others, others might pay attention to learning how to be patient when trying to problem-solve or how to help others debug. Some might use mindfulness for helping children work through the frustration of trying to debug with little success, and others might use thank-you cards to acknowledge the generous spirit of helping each other problem-solve.

The CAL curriculum juxtaposes coding and literacy as powerful tools of communication, creative expression, and meaning-making. Each unit contains a minimum of twelve, one-hour lessons or a maximum of twenty-four, forty-five minutes lessons, centered on coding projects about books, both fiction and nonfiction. For example, fictional storybooks include *Where the Wild Things Are* by Maurice Sendak or *There Was an Old Lady Who Swallowed a Fly* by Simms Taback. Nonfiction books tell the story of a pioneer in computer science, such as *Ada Lovelace, Poet of Science: The First Computer Programmer* by Diane Stanley or *A Computer Called Katherine: How Katherine Johnson Helped Put America on the Moon* by Suzanne Slade. Teachers are encouraged to substitute any of these with their own favorite books as long as they have a clear sequencing of events.

The CAL curriculum presents a scope and sequence of coding skills and content, a structure based on powerful ideas from computer science, and a learning pathway. At the same time, it is designed to be flexible, and the lessons are adaptable to better integrate with the rest of the teaching. The timing can be adjusted to make lessons longer or shorter to better suit the curricular needs of different schools. While the content is organized in terms of powerful ideas of computer science, explicit connections are made in each of the units to early childhood literacy. In addition, opportunities to engage with math and other subject areas are presented.

Constructionism has not always viewed a predetermined curriculum favorably, as it is doubtful it can support all children's personal interests. My perspective is that a well-designed curriculum that can be adapted and modified is a wonderful tool for equity in education. First, it ensures that the targeted powerful ideas of the computer science discipline will be covered in a developmentally appropriate way, despite differing depths of understanding across different teachers. Second, it keeps the playfulness and encouragement of open exploration. Third, it highlights that the coding activities must support socioemotional growth and the development of character strengths.

Jerome Bruner, the influential American psychologist who made significant contributions to cognitive learning theory, among other things, wrote in his 1960s seminal book *The Process of Education* that *"curriculum of a subject should be determined by the most fundamental understanding that can be achieved of the underlying principles that give structure to that subject."* Seymour Papert called these powerful ideas: such are deeply rooted in a discipline, are personally useful, inherently interconnected with other disciplines, and are grounded in intuitive knowledge that a child has internalized over a long period of time. For example, in mathematics, the concepts of zero or addition or estimation are all powerful ideas. In literacy, there are the notions of grammar and syntax. In coding, there are algorithms and conditionals.

In his 1980s book *Mindstorms: Children, Computers, and Powerful Ideas*, Papert wrote that *"when one enters a new domain of knowledge, one initially encounters a crowd of new ideas. Good learners are able to pick out those which are powerful."* While this is the goal, the reality is that people need to learn how to become good learners. Most teachers do not have the time to become good learners of computer science. Thus, they cannot identify its powerful ideas, nor can they make it developmentally appropriate. That is when a curriculum becomes empowering; it already did the work of picking up the important ideas from a crowd of many.

The CAL curriculum identifies in each lesson powerful ideas from both computer science and literacy. These ideas are aligned with federal Common Core literacy standards and K–12 computer science frameworks so that teachers can meet federal and state requirements. While each district, state, or country has its own specific frameworks, the powerful ideas cover most of them. Furthermore, the curriculum is designed in such a way that localization is possible by proposing a palette of virtues with universal values that can be adapted and modified to particular cultural, social, and religious contexts.

Powerful Ideas

In my previous book *Coding as a Playground*, I wrote extensively about seven powerful ideas from the discipline of computer science that I have identified as being developmentally appropriate: algorithms, design process, representation, debugging, control structures, modularity, and hardware/software systems. These ideas capture some of the core concepts and skills a child can acquire when learning to program and thinking computationally (figure 5.1).

The CAL curriculum organizes each of its lessons around these powerful ideas and provides opportunities for engaging in unplugged games, warm-up activities, and coding projects to explore them. As children grow, the ideas grow with them. For example, understanding algorithmic thinking in prekindergarten might focus on linear sequencing, while in second grade it extends to loops. Children can understand that within a sequence, there are patterns that repeat themselves.

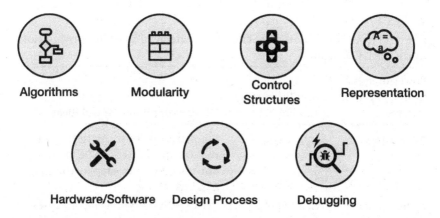

Algorithms   **Modularity**   **Control Structures**   **Representation**

Hardware/Software   **Design Process**   **Debugging**

Figure 5.1
Powerful, developmentally appropriate ideas from computer science

In addition, CAL presents powerful ideas from literacy: the writing process, recalling, summarizing and sequencing, using illustrative and descriptive language, recognizing literary devices such as repetition and foreshadowing, and using reading strategies such as predicting, summarizing, and evaluating. These ideas are informed by literacy frameworks and research by experts in the early years.

While the CAL curriculum might focus on a particular programming environment, such as ScratchJr or KIBO, the powerful ideas, if they are indeed powerful, remain the same. That is true for coding and for reading and writing in most languages. Furthermore, these ideas can also be encountered when engaging in low-tech games or unplugged activities aimed at promoting computational thinking and alphabetical literacy. They can even inspire the development of cartoons and media for children. For example, for some time now I have been serving as content director for a series to be aired in 2023 by PBS Kids (Public Broadcasting Service) in the United States. Cute, animated Wombats encounter these powerful ideas as they face new adventures.

Table 5.1 presents both sets of powerful ideas, from computer science and from literacy, and describes their intersection. One

Table 5.1

Powerful Ideas from Computer Science and Literacy Placed in Conversation in the CAL Curriculum

Powerful ideas from computer science	Powerful ideas from literacy	Connecting the powerful ideas
Algorithms	Sequencing	Emphasis on "order matters" and that complex tasks can be broken down into step-by-step instructions in a logical way.
Design process	Writing process	Creative, iterative, cyclic processes that involve imagining, planning, making, revising, and sharing, with different starting points.
Representation	Alphabet and letter-sound correspondence	Symbols have different attributes (color, shape, sound, etc.) to represent something else.
Debugging	Editing and audience awareness	Systematic analysis, testing, and evaluation to improve communication to the intended audience (computer or person). Whenever miscommunication occurs, the programmer or writer uses a variety of strategies to solve the problem.
Control structures	Literary devices	Advanced strategies to communicate a set of ideas using repetition, patterns, conditionals, and events.
Modularity	Phonological awareness	Decomposition, or breaking down a complex task into smaller tasks and reusing those new modules.
Hardware and software	Tools of communication and language	Communicating abstract ideas through tangible means. Just like how hardware and software work together, expressing thoughts through language requires a medium for communicating to the outside world, such as the spoken or written word.

curricular domain is used to leverage the other. Examples include when children encounter algorithmic thinking, they are also exploring sequencing and storytelling; when they engage in the design process, they make active connections to the writing process; and when they set to debug their ill-functioning programs, they tap into revising strategies that share similarities with the systematic editing of their writing.

There are significant differences between using programming languages and natural languages for expressing ourselves. CAL does not ignore them. However, as an integrated curriculum, the focus is on shared practices: the creation of projects, either through coding or through writing; the creative design process involved in making these projects; the need to revise and fix them at each step of the way; and the sharing of final projects with others as a way to express our individuality, interests, passions, and identities.

All seven ideas are powerful. However, in the coding playground the idea of design process calls for special attention. CAL invites children to use language, programming, and alphabetical written language to create, express, and communicate. That requires a process and an audience. It involves realizing there is another: a computer or a robot that needs to "understand" our ideas or a person who needs to read our composition.

In our pedagogy and curriculum, awareness of audience and design process also provides an opportunity for developing our palette of virtues. We engage in the hard work of creating something we are proud of and ready to share with others. Working with the design process involves mastery of skills and systematic revisions, creativity to come up with an idea, persistence, and patience to stick with it until having a sharable product. Generosity is important to give constructive feedback, and optimism is crucial for completing our project. Gratitude is necessary to acknowledge those who helped us in the process, and fairness is essential for assessing how we are doing.

For example, when programming KIBO to dance the Hokey Pokey, some children may spend a long time in the testing phase, dancing and singing together along with their robot until they get the timing for their program right. Once they receive feedback, they may want to go back to testing to include a dance step they missed. Others may choose to plan each step of their Hokey Pokey program in a design journal before testing out any ideas. As children become more familiar with the design process, they develop the ability to iteratively create and refine their work, to give and receive feedback to others, and to continually improve a project based on experimenting and testing. This leads to iterative improvement, involves perseverance, and has strong associations with some aspects of executive functions, such as self-control, planning, prioritizing, and organization, all of which are important in our lives.

We use the design process not only when coding and writing but also in most endeavors in which expression is the final outcome and there is a genuine concern about "the other," about an audience that needs to interact with or use our creation. Across different disciplines, each design process has a distinct flavor. The level of granularity and detail in each of its steps varies according to the goal it serves. The design process involved in engineering a highway is not the same process required for painting a wall. However, in both of these examples, there is a sense of responsibility associated with the process of creation.

In previous work, I described the design process involved in coding as consisting of six steps that are easy for young children to remember: 1) ask a question, 2) imagine an idea, 3) plan and brainstorm, 4) create a prototype, 5) test and improve the prototype, and 6) share the final product. At DevTech, we even wrote a song about it to the tune of "Twinkle, Twinkle, Little Star" to facilitate memorization in the early childhood classroom.

We chose to visualize the design process as an infinite loop involving these six steps (figure 5.2). Although there is a defined

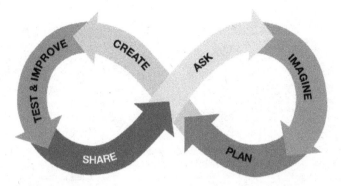

Figure 5.2
The design process

sequence, each step is interrelated with the others. One is likely to go back and forth between steps or to miss some of them rather than follow a linear path. In the coding playground, designing is a messy, creative activity. We do not expect children to neatly follow each of the steps. Thus, we must offer multiple opportunities to experience the design process as an iterative cycle with different entry points.

Throughout the steps of the design process, the I–Thou and I–It relationships described by Buber take on a different meaning. There is an interplay between the I who creates and the Thou who provides feedback. The I who revises and the Thou who brainstorms. The I who fixes and the Thou who tests. The I who programs and the Thou who uses. The It, the prototype or product of our creative activity, becomes a vehicle for nurturing relationships. Within this Buberian framework, the last step of the design process, sharing the final product, becomes both an act of generosity and gratitude, an opportunity for deep human connection.

With its focus on both coding and literacy, the CAL curriculum explores how the design process and the writing process are parallel to one another. The design process is used to create computational projects, while the writing process is used to create texts (figure 5.3).

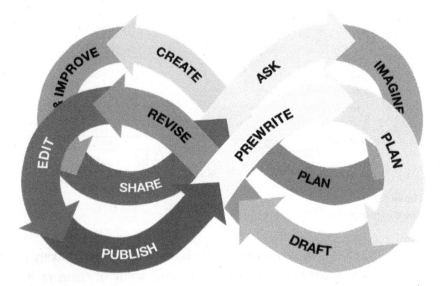

Figure 5.3
Alignment of the design and the writing process

Both require an audience that becomes active by interpreting the text or by interacting with the computational artifact. Both involve responsible creation and awareness about others. Skillful teachers can explore the similarities and differences in the process of creation in two learning environments that initially might seem very different from each other, such as the writer's workshop and the coding playground, but share pedagogical strategies and a sense of ethical responsibility toward our creations.

While the teaching of different design processes is similar regardless of the programming language used because it focuses on revision and iteration, the teaching of the symbol system, syntax, and grammar vary across languages. Like natural languages, different programming languages have their own characteristics. For example, Spanish has the letter ñ, which does not exist in English. Similarly, the KIBO programming language includes sensors, which are absent in ScratchJr. ScratchJr has the possibility to program speed, which is not found in KIBO.

Each CAL curriculum addresses the uniqueness of each programming language as it relates to the core powerful ideas of computer science. For example, while both CAL-KIBO and CAL-ScratchJr focus on the powerful idea of software/hardware systems and discuss how to take care of materials, the specifics are language dependent. The CAL-KIBO curriculum teaches about sensors and makes explicit connections between human, animal, and artificial sensors. In contrast, the CAL-ScratchJr curriculum focuses on navigating the interface, plugging, unplugging, and charging batteries.

Despite the variation of coding tools, all curriculum units follow a similar structure: warm-up games to playfully introduce ideas, coding activities to solidify skills, structured challenges to practice, creative explorations to tinker and expand skills, off-screen unplugged games to promote social interactions and movement, reading and writing activities, and technology circles to share and reflect. The curriculum is composed of individual, small group, and whole classroom activities. Some of these can happen in centers; they can be located in specific areas around the classroom so that children can work in small groups or independently. Lessons strongly incorporate one or many of the six Cs of PTD by promoting content creation, creativity, communication, collaboration, choices of conduct, and community building. In addition, there are games and activities designed to reinforce each of the values in the palette of virtues.

Throughout the curriculum, students keep a design journal. While kindergarten students are invited to draw or voice record their ideas in the journal, older students are expected to write according to their literacy level. Sometimes written journals are used to assess literacy skills, and they are often included in the portfolio of projects that children can take home to their families. The journals make learning visible. The culmination of each CAL unit involves a multi-day, open-ended project to share with family and friends. This provides an opportunity to celebrate the children's hard work and thank all of those who contributed to the their learning process.

A Teacher's Perspective

It is early morning in Norfolk, Virginia. A community room is awoken by the shuffling of chairs, the connection of a projector, and the smell of coffee. Soon enough, the first teachers start to trickle into the room. On a day that would have been a holiday, teachers from eight different schools are attending a day-long CAL-KIBO training. Slowly, they greet each other and sort themselves into their school groups. The room comes to a hush as Madhu Govind, a doctoral student in my DevTech lab, welcomes them with a smile, introduces the research team, and asks everyone, "What are your initial thoughts and expectations for today?"

Encouraged to express with honesty, teachers go around the room: "I can't wait to bring robotics into my second grade." "I am not sure if it will work with my class. We have many children for whom English is their second language." "I do not feel comfortable with technology." "I barely know how to use my iPhone. How will I learn KIBO?" The answers are as varied as the personalities of the participating teachers, and emotions such as hesitancy and uncertainty fill the room.

Once feelings are shared, the DevTech team starts the professional development. They show the KIBO robot, explain how it works, and invite teachers to program it to dance the Hokey Pokey. This is an opportunity for grown-ups to become children again, to display their creativity in a fun context without the pressure to both learn a new tool and figure out how to integrate it into the curriculum. After sharing their Hokey Pokey dances, teachers feel more relaxed. There is laughter in the room. There is trial and error. There is silliness and cooperation. The palette of virtues is on full display.

After this hands-on introductory KIBO experience, attention is shifted to pedagogy and curriculum. Slowly, the pedagogy of CAL is introduced as well as the PTD framework and its six Cs. Questions and answers are discussed. When everyone seems to be on board, Govind asks the teachers to be quiet. It is time to play again, but this time it will be with both books and robots.

Teachers are invited to choose one of two books, *Where the Wild Things Are* and *There Was an Old Lady Who Swallowed a Fly*, as their inspiration for a KIBO project. The room is filled with chatter and collaboration, making teachers aware of the importance of communication when coding. The activity in the room ranges from handling scissors that snip away at construction paper to scanning endless sequences of blocks to retell the stories. After the final warning, teachers came together for the first technology circle. Each group presents their KIBO decorations and the reasoning behind their choice of programming blocks to recreate the sequences in the books.

For the last few years, the DevTech Research Group has been collaborating with Angela R. de Mik and the Norfolk Public Schools in southeastern Virginia in kindergarten through second grades. Later, this section discusses a vignette depicting the experience of teachers who implemented the CAL-KIBO curriculum in eight schools through a grant from the US Department of Defense.

The CAL approach requires that teachers understand the pedagogy of why and how coding is taught as another language and not only the technical aspects of computer programming and KIBO robotics. Furthermore, professional development must appeal to the emotional experience and not only the intellectual challenge. If teachers love what they learn in their training, they are more likely to put the effort into bringing it to their students.

Educators are constantly inundated with new initiatives, curricula, and programs. This can feel exhausting and breeds a disposition of skepticism. The more experienced the teachers, the truer this can be, as they have seen fads pop up and fade out throughout their careers. "When you're a teacher, it's always something new. Someone always wants to tell us something new that we need to do. When we first found out that we would be coding, it sounded intimidating, we didn't know anything about it," described one of the Norfolk teachers. "I think the training kind of eased our minds, and then actually doing it and seeing how much kids loved it and the benefit that it had, was great."

Throughout the curriculum, different activities integrate computer science and literacy by using the book *Where the Wild Things Are* by Maurice Sendak. For example, in lesson 6 (What Did Max Sense), they read about how the protagonist of the book, a little boy named Max, uses his five senses. This activity leads into the introduction of the various sensors in the KIBO robotic kit, where the older children are exposed to the wider variety of sensors. While in the younger grades children talk about the difference between human, animal, and technological sensors, in the second grade, teachers guide a discussion comparing the "poetic" language used in the story to describe Max's senses and the contrasting command language in the KIBO programming language to describe sensing.

For the final project, children imagine and discuss what was happening in the wild rumpus described in the book and write their own ideas as to what a wild rumpus robotics dance would look like. While in the younger classrooms, children are invited to draw their dances in their journals, in the older grades, they are given prompts to write using descriptive language. At the end, they all decorate their KIBOs and program them to dance the wild rumpus.

During the professional development day in Norfolk, teachers themselves created a wild rumpus dance and shared it with each other (figure 5.4). For many, this was the highlight of the day, as it incorporated dance, arts, crafts, and music, turning the robotics class into a coding playground.

Figure 5.4
Wild rumpus characters created by Norfolk teachers

In addition to the one-day professional development, prior to working with their students, teachers had multiple opportunities for ongoing professional learning. This consisted of lesson slide decks, video tutorials, coaching calls with my DevTech team, and additional in-person support provided by the district's instructional technology resource technicians.

While some teachers were more successful than others, all of the schools were able to complete the implementation of the CAL-KIBO curriculum, approximately twice a week for a period spanning six to eight weeks. Naturally, the more advanced lessons in the curriculum were more difficult and time-consuming. Teachers who were successful in completing them consistently met with their colleagues to discuss plans, took advantage of opportunities to practice with KIBO on their own, and were able to adapt the lessons to serve the needs of their own students. The teachers who struggled would have benefited from more time spent on training, developing their own KIBO skills, and taking advantages of the provided resources. Teachers who had many students with not enough floor space for them to work on or had rigid grade-level schedules faced more challenging experiences.

During the CAL-KIBO project, we collected multiple types of data from teachers and students at various points in the curriculum. We used the data to answer the following research questions: How did our CAL-KIBO curriculum promote students' coding and computational thinking skills? What is the relationship between students' coding and computational thinking and their literacy and math skills? How did teachers react to KIBO and our CAL approach? What did teachers learn during the training and intervention? What factors impacted teachers' ability to integrate coding into their classrooms? In the last chapter of this book, Resources, you can find a link to further readings and peer-reviewed publications with the findings.

Overall, students and teachers had a generally positive experience with CAL-KIBO. For many teachers, the hands-on nature of the robot was a welcomed addition to their classrooms. For example, Selma expressed "I learned that coding doesn't just involve sitting in front of a computer and typing things; it actually involves using your mind and talking things out." Selma showed a great skill at integrating dance and movement into the CAL-KIBO curriculum. However, other teachers struggled with the logistics of so many tangible materials. Carla shared with us that "things were messy, the KIBOs were in and out of the classroom, and things got mixed up, so I color-coded mine." Carla complained that keeping track of the materials added more work for her.

The organization of KIBO blocks and modules presented its own set of challenges, particularly shifting materials between classrooms and managing clean-up time. Some teachers developed strategies such as creating a clear rotational system with fellow teachers, having select students in charge of KIBO clean-up, and keeping three to four KIBOs in their own classrooms at all times. For some, managing the KIBO materials was an opportunity to put into practice the palette of virtues; for others, it felt as if coding was just taking time away from teaching required content.

During the teacher interviews and conversations with the leadership, we learned that classroom and school contexts clearly played an important role in the success of the CAL-KIBO curriculum. For instance, manageable classroom sizes, flexible schedules to accommodate KIBO at least twice a week, and enough KIBO kits for students to work in small groups proved to be the most effective.

Teachers varied in how they responded to the CAL pedagogy. Even the most resistant teachers felt that the curriculum reinforced oral communication and collaboration, which is very important in early childhood. However, in terms of literacy, there was a distinct trend: teachers who understood literacy instruction as singularly focused on discrete skills (e.g., phonics, punctuation) were less open to the CAL-KIBO curriculum and to the overall integration of computer science and literacy. For example, some teachers complained the writing activities embedded in CAL "aren't going to meet the student's needs for writing or reading as required by state standards" and that CAL "does not reinforce capitalization and grammar."

Conversely, teachers who understood literacy in broader terms and saw metacognitive ideas about reading and writing as essential to the development of robust literacy abilities (e.g., communication, creative expression, interpretation, telling and retelling skills, awareness of audience and purpose) were very welcoming to the curriculum. For example, Jenna expressed how happy she was with the inclusion of writing alongside coding: "The editing piece to me was very strong, going back and fixing things and not getting frustrated when you face challenges and really looking at it as something else to figure out." Pat shared that "the parallels between the engineer design and the writing process is a solid connection that the kids can see and understand."

During our analyses of writing samples in students' design journals, we observed that the CAL-KIBO curriculum appealed to students of all abilities. We saw this trend repeatedly throughout this project. Students' writing in the context of CAL-KIBO was substantively different from their standardized writing tests. In addition, when writing about their robotic projects, students were often more creative writers than when writing for other subjects.

Coding Stages

Curriculum and assessment display two sides of the same coin. When we teach, we want to know whether children are learning. If they are not, we need to revise our instruction. Assessment provides opportunities to adjust and modify teaching practices and to gather the needed information to communicate with parents.

There are different ways to assess student's learning in early childhood. Observing children's behaviors, listening to their stories and reasoning, and analyzing the work they produce, through portfolios, are popular. Other methods involve testing to identify challenges and special needs. Sometimes these assessments are done by an outsider to the classroom and others by the classroom teachers. Each of these methods poses it owns challenges to monitor students' progress. However, they have been around for a long time, and many lessons have been learned from their standardization.

When it comes to coding in early childhood, that is not the case. Few assessments have been validated and children, who are just learning to read and write, cannot complete individual worksheets or exams. Furthermore, in most early childhood classrooms, due to the lack of access to technological devices, children work in groups. While the resulting projects can be assessed, it can be challenging to evaluate a child's individual learning trajectory when she has been working in a team.

The DevTech Research Group developed new instruments to capture the individuality of children's learning to code in expressive ways. In the last chapter of this book, Resources, you will find links to a rubric to evaluate both KIBO and ScratchJr projects with a CAL perspective as well as links to TechCheck, a platform-independent unplugged validated instrument to capture computational thinking. You will also find the Coding Stages Assessment (CSA) for both KIBO and ScratchJr. CSA is a validated cumulative assessment that identifies the coding level attained by each student. It can be used when CAL curriculum is completed or at any time teachers or researchers want to know the coding level a child is at.

CSA captures not only mastery of syntax and grammar of the programming language but also the child's ability to engage in the expressive and purposeful usage of the programming language. What is unique about the CSA assessment is both the approach in which it is couched (CAL) and its development and validation process: we combined design-based research with psychometric methods to create an instrument that builds on the pedagogical and design traditions of decades of work and has good measurement properties.

Often, I am asked by teachers and parents how to know if their child is learning to code. They appreciate that our approach encourages children to create their own projects, to express themselves, and to follow their true interests, but this sometimes makes it difficult to truly assess their skills. "Is my daughter choosing to always program her characters with simple motion blocks in ScratchJr because she likes it or because she doesn't know how to use other blocks?" "Why do my students never use the passing of messages blocks when programming their dialogues in ScratchJr? Is it because they find there is no need to or because they do not understand how to use them?" "Is my son avoiding the light sensor with the if command in KIBO because he doesn't want it for his project or because he can't get it to work?" These are many of the questions that parents and educators ask themselves when looking at their children's projects.

Over many years, in the DevTech Research Group we also asked those questions. We observed young children coding expressively with KIBO and ScratchJr. We collected and analyzed data, interviewed children and teachers, and found patterns and regularities, transition points, and dead ends. We also read the work of other researchers, who in their own fields of study faced similar challenges in assessing children's stage development and learning trajectories in authentic contexts.

For example, we looked carefully at the work on developmental stages of reading conducted by Harvard professor Jeanne Chall in the late 60s. She was among the first researchers to describe reading as a developmental process and to identify several stages. We also looked at the work of Douglas Clements and Julie Sarama, now at the University of Denver, on mathematical learning progressions in early childhood. And we looked at the work of the Argentinian educational psychologists Emilia Ferreira and Ana Terbosky on the psychogenesis of written language. All of their fascinating research shows that once educators understand developmental progressions based on research-based evidence and can sequence their curriculum activities based on them, the learning of new ideas and skills can be developmentally appropriate and effective for young children. The same is true for coding.

We identified five coding stages, or developmental progressions, that children move through when creating their own personally meaningful projects using a developmentally appropriate programming language. These coding stages are emergent, coding and decoding, fluency, new knowledge, and purposefulness. While in my early work I had presented six stages, further research and empirical studies with hundreds of children with the CSA showed us that multiple perspectives, the stage I discussed in my earlier work as the fifth stage, was indeed the same as purposefulness. Thus, our current model of coding stages has five stages. The transition between all stages might not happen without scaffolded instruction. While learning to code is possible by just tinkering and exploring the coding playground, figuring out some of the syntax and grammar and progressing through all stages until mastering the last stage, purposefulness, might require explicit teaching.

The choice of the term *stages* is influenced by Piaget's work. However, our coding stages depart from Piaget in an important way. We are not engaging in a universal effort to explain a naturally occurring phenomenon, like Piaget's cognitive development stages do. Coding stages are a blueprint to describe a learning path for young children engaged with a developmentally appropriate programming language. They are levels or benchmarks of growth that represent distinct ways of mastering creative, expressive coding.

Traditionally, developmental progressions are seen as sequential, orderly, and cumulative. However, development is fluid and interconnected. Coding stages are interconnected and not fixed or fully linear. Depending on the level of instruction received, and the degree of a child's curiosity to explore on her own, a child can jump or never reach a particular stage. For example, using the ScratchJr programming language, children in the earlier stages might be able to select motion blocks but might not understand how to create an animation connecting those blocks. Although the coding stages are not universal, they can be observed across different programming languages.

The coding stages have some hierarchy based on syntax and grammar—mastery of simpler structures or commands (e.g., start/ end) occurs before mastery of more complex structures (e.g., if statement). The five sequential stages capture a growing skill set with a specific programming language: at each of these levels of attainment, a child can create an expressive computational project with growing complexity. Identifying a child as being at one of these stages indicates that she has gained creative programming knowledge; she has learned the grammar and syntax of the programming language, not only to solve a puzzle but to also create an expressive project.

The last stage, purposefulness, captures the ability to use the programming language for expression while mastering all of its

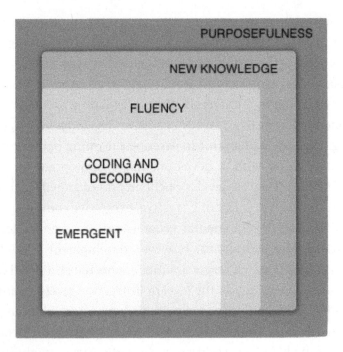

Figure 5.5
The five coding stages. From light to dark, the color gradient shows a typical child's directional progression with coding. However, the purposefulness stage breaks this linear progression as elements can be found at each stage.

elements (figure 5.5). This stage captures intentionality and the ability to tell a story about the created project, to reflect and engage in metacognition. For example, a child in the last stage, purposefulness, can not only code in a rapid and efficient manner at high levels of abstraction requiring skill and flexibility by using all commands but also design her personally engaging projects applying that knowledge. The focus is on expression and communication, not only on problem-solving or computational thinking abilities.

I developed the concept of coding stages to serve three goals. The first goal is to guide the development of coding curriculum and the scope and sequence of instructional activities matched to each of the levels. The second is to evaluate children's mastery of coding with a developmentally appropriate programming language, and the third is to advance a developmental approach for the nascent field of early childhood computer science that includes the use of validated research instruments.

Table 5.2 describes the five coding stages identified over decades of working with young children with KIBO and ScratchJr. Given that both are introductory programming languages, it is possible for young children to reach the more complex stages that would be difficult to attain with more sophisticated programming languages. We have not done the work to explore whether these five coding stages transfer to other programming languages and pedagogical approaches for young children.

A Window into Their World: The Missing Audience

Sarah looked intently at the picture of a cartoon turtle and fox hugging. She tapped her pencil against her writing journal. Soon, with a spark of inspiration, she began to write a story about it. She wrote in silence, her head buried in her writing. Five minutes later she looked up. "Done," she said. Dr. Ziva Hassenfeld, then a postdoc in my DevTech Research Group and now an assistant professor at Brandeis University, asked Sarah to read her composition out loud. Sarah read her story with difficulty. She encountered grammatical and syntactical errors, which she orally fixed as she read, but she did not edit her writing.

A week later, during "writer's workshop," Sarah continued working on her turtle and fox story. After six minutes, she declared herself done. She reread her composition and declined an invitation to revise the writing. The following week, after reading what she had composed in the previous two weeks, Sarah declared, "This is the story, but . . ." She pointed to many words. "This is not how

Table 5.2

The Five Coding Stages

Coding Stage	Description
1. Emergent	• The child recognizes that technologies are human engineered and designed with a variety of purposes. • The child understands the concept of symbolization and representation (i.e., a command is not the behavior but represents the behavior). • The child understands what a programming language and the purpose of its use is (knows that a basic sequence and control structure exists). • The child is familiar with the basics of the interface (turn the tool on and off and correctly interact). This is a beginner's stage.
2. Coding and decoding	• The child understands sequencing matters and that the order in which commands are put together generates different behaviors. • The child has learned a limited set of symbols and grammar rules to create a simple project. • The child can correctly create simple programs with simple cause and effect commands. • The child can identify and fix grammatical errors in the code. • The child performs simple debugging through trial and error. • The child engages in goal-oriented command exploration. The most growth can be seen at this stage. Children learn the basics of the programming language and understand it can serve to create projects of their choice.
3. Fluency	• The child has mastered the syntax of the programming language and can correctly create programs. • The child is personally motivated to create complex programs. • The child understands how to distinguish and fix logical errors in the code. • The child is beginning to be strategic in debugging. This stage is characterized by the child moving from a "learning to code" to a "coding to learn" creative stance.

Table 5.2 (continued)

Coding Stage	Description
4. New knowledge	• The child understands how to combine multiple control structures and create nested programs that achieve complex sequencing.
	• The child engages in more goal-oriented logical exploration with their programs.
	• The child is personally motivated to create complex programs.
	• The child is strategic in debugging and has developed strategies.
	• The child learns how to learn new commands or novel uses of the interface.
	This stage is characterized by the child's ability to use her knowledge to create a personally meaningful project and, if needed, acquire new knowledge on her own to meet the demands of the project.
5. Purposefulness	• The child can skillfully create complex programs for her needs and purpose.
	• The child understands how to analyze, synthesize, and translate abstract concepts into code and vice versa.
	• The child can identify multiple ways to translate abstract concepts into code.
	• The child understands how to create programs that involve the user's input.
	• The child can create multiple programs that interact with one another.
	• The child can debug multiple control structures.
	This stage is characterized by the child being able to code in a rapid and efficient manner at high levels of abstraction requiring skill and flexibility and applying those skills to create a personally meaningful project. A child who reaches this stage has mastered all of the commands, grammar, and syntax of the programming language and has the ability to express herself through the project she creates.

you spell this stuff," she reflected. "It is confusing when I read it, but if I tell it to you, you will get it." And then, instead of fixing her writing, she meticulously crossed the whole thing out—line by line, page by page. Writing was hard for this seven-year-old girl but revising it was even harder. It would take less effort to start all over again.

Sarah's teacher described Sarah as being right on target with her writing skills, maybe even a little bit more advanced than the rest of her second-grade classmates. In the phonics lessons, Sarah was in the highest-level group. She hit the specific benchmarks for spelling, decoding, and basic grammar. She was able to recognize errors but was not willing to put the extra work to revise and edit them.

This attitude in the writing class was in sharp contrast with Sarah's behavior in the coding class. On her first coding day, she started a ScratchJr animated version of the turtle and fox story, loosely based on her original writing composition. By the second time she met with Dr. Hassenfeld, Sarah had a programming project displaying a conversation between the two characters. She tested her program often and found many problems to fix. Without hesitation, Sarah debugged her animated story with ease and eagerness, and she debugged logical errors as well as fixed the aesthetics of her program. She did not choose to delete everything and start over when things did not work. Quite the opposite: she persevered and kept working. This was in marked contrast with her writing experience. When Dr. Hassenfeld asked her about her different attitudes, Sarah expressed that revising writing requires a lot of energy with little in return. Instead, debugging is more rewarding: "You can see it working."

Before observing Sarah's attitude when debugging her code, the teacher had assumed that Sarah was not trying hard at writing and was why she would not sit down and spend the needed time and effort revising her story. However, after observing Sarah's high level of personal investment in fixing her coding project, she realized there must be another reason. "CAL is aligned so well with writing," explained Sarah's teacher. "Each day with each lesson the kids are writing and programming. And there is also lots of reading. We read them a book and they read other people's instructions and projects and stuff like that. They learn to improve their writing and revise and edit. I think it is aligned well, but it is not working for Sarah. She is shining in her ScratchJr project, but she is not revising her writing."

After working with Sarah for an extended period, Dr. Hassenfeld discovered what was troubling Sarah. One of her biggest challenges was the imaginative leap required to engage in the revision process in writing. Sarah, the all-knowing author, had to transition to become an unknowing reader. She had a difficult time switching perspective. Instead, while coding, she did not need to switch. She could remain an all-knowing programmer and fix what did not work: the syntactical and logical errors.

ScratchJr gave her specific feedback (it works or it does not), and Sarah's job was to address the problems. In contrast, when writing, she had to switch to become an audience, a reader. As a writer, she understood what was happening, but as a reader things did not always make sense. To fix her writing, she needed to switch back and forth between being the author and the audience, which proved exhausting for Sarah. Writing demands to make things explicit, and that is a lot of work if there is not an authentic motivation to put the effort. What would she do with her writing? It would be one more piece of paper in her messy portfolio to take home at the end of the year.

In conversations with Dr. Hassenfeld, Sarah's teacher realized that although Sarah was performing well in the standardized reading and writing assessments, these were not capturing her lack of motivation for editing. She put in place different strategies for helping Sarah and other children like her. For example, she engaged children in other compositional activities that also involve a revision process, such as art and music activities, and asked her students to vocalize their thoughts as they revised. She also went over the design and writing process again and taught the children how to make books to take their stories home to share with their parents.

When interviewed, Sarah's teacher expressed that "for me, debugging and revising are connected conceptually and pedagogically. Now, my students are increasingly seeing that debugging in coding compositions is the means by which clarity is achieved and that this skill is related to editing in written composition. However, they need to have an authentic reason to want to put the effort." The motivation comes easily with coding because children are excited to show their projects to others. And for that to happen, projects need to work. In contrast, with writing, the audience can fill the gaps if there are syntactic and grammatical errors and still appreciate the story.

In the coding playground, the hope is that by working through the different steps of the design process, from an initial idea to a finished product to share with others, motivation is promoted by creating an authentic learning community. This community will sustain the child in the process of working hard at both coding and writing.

6

Coding Character

Joan (five years old): I want to make a good robot. What can it do?

Researcher: Why don't you make the robot help you store your toys?

Joan (five years old): My mom will help me. My robot will cook so my mom can clean up with me.

The Media Lab at MIT is a very special place to learn. During the late 90s, when I did my masters and PhD, the lab had lots of funding, opportunities for cutting-edge research, and possibilities to collaborate with industries and organizations to take our prototypes out of the lab and make a societal impact. What I appreciated the most were the people: individual stars and collaborative peers who were creative and skilled, supportive, and challenging.

My background was not in computer science, like most of my classmates. Technical classes were difficult for me. I had ideas but needed help implementing them. I spent hours working with my peers. Sometimes I would get recommendations for books to read and lectures to attend, while other times I needed help debugging code or writing a technical job description to hire a bright undergraduate student to assist me. Almost twenty years after my graduation, I still remember the intellectual generosity of the many students I interacted with at the MIT Media Lab.

For me, going to school meant problem solving with others. In that context, the character of the others mattered a lot. Some were helpful and others not. Some wanted to collaborate, and others wanted to compete. Some pushed boundaries so that each other's work would become better. Others sought personal glory and the press. Although we were solving technical challenges, character strength rather than technical expertise was the best predictor of the quality of the experience.

The values we cherish, and how we behave, permeate every aspect of our lives. However, both identity and character are not fixed constructs. People change, people learn, and people develop. Good character can be cultivated. In this book, I am proposing that the coding playground can be another space to promote character development and positive behaviors. Furthermore, over the past twenty-five years, I have explored how to intentionally design these spaces.

We live in a society where concepts of self, family, community, and what is right and wrong are constantly changing. At the same time, there are values that seem to hold true regardless of historical periods or social contexts. Justice, honesty, and generosity are a few examples. Our complex and pluralistic societies face the challenge of welcoming diversity of perspectives, cultures, ethnicities and religions while embracing universal values that enable people to coexist in peace, seek prosperity, and respect fundamental human rights. The term *values* suggest the importance or worth of something. Values are anchored to traditions and a sense of belonging, to identity and emotions, to morality and civics, and to character strengths and virtuous deeds.

Over the centuries, the religions of the Book—Judaism, Christianity, and Islam—have provided a moral code of conduct and an invitation to interpret it. Unfortunately, as religions became institutionalized and sought political power, the ethical code was sometimes forgotten and the moral teachings misused. In the East, Confucius developed theories of proper human behavior and social organization, which today would be called ethical and political philosophy. Buddhism focused on lovingkindness and compassion for all beings and offered a framework for healing the suffering of the world. In ancient Greece, Socrates strived to live an "examined life," and his disciples Plato and Aristotle created a logic system for reasoning, the foundation of what we now call critical thinking. In *The Republic*, Plato was concerned with the character and the mind of the young Greek; the final goal of education was as moral as it was intellectual.

From theology to philosophy and from psychology to sociology, competing and conflicting theories study values, virtues, and character. Education is charged with engaging in the deliberate effort to advance them. Religious institutions always understood that part of their mission was to educate people about values and virtues. When the new institution of school emerged in the wake of the Industrial Revolution, there was a need to make the learner's experience uniform and universal through a standardized curriculum. Where was then the place for values? Which values were to be taught?

In countries like the United States, the first schools were founded by New England puritans who believed the moral code resided in the Bible. As waves of immigrants came to the country from the mid-nineteenth century forward, the orthodoxy of the schools came under scrutiny. A growing movement advocating the separation of church and state pushed for distancing public schools from moral education, which was so deeply associated with religion. Some educators became proponents of "value-free" schooling, ignoring the fact that it is impossible to create a school devoid of ethical issues and controversies. Others explored different approaches that led civics education and character development to emerge.

While the term *moral* carries religious overtones for many, the word *character* speaks to good habits and civic virtues, which hold a community together in harmony. A person who exhibits personal qualities desirable by society might be considered to have good character. One of the purposes of education is developing these good personal qualities. However, proponents of character education are far from agreement as to what "good" means or what qualities are desirable.

Scientists are developing research programs to better understand this question. However, since character involves both personality and behavioral components, it is a challenging problem. With no clinical definitions, it is difficult to measure if an individual has a particular strength of character, or if a school program can improve it. Some efforts, such as the *Character Strengths and Virtues* handbook published in 2004, attempts to classify and develop a common vocabulary of measurable positive traits. The handbook classifies twenty-four character strengths under six broad virtues that consistently emerge across history and cultures: wisdom, courage, humanity, justice, temperance, and transcendence. The development of classifications such as this one allows us to better study in a scientific way how people live a good life and how to implement educational programs to promote it.

Over the decades, many programs have been put in place. However, without validated measurement instruments, it is hard to research their effectiveness and impact. Each of these programs has their own pedagogical tools and methodologies, success stories, anecdotal evidence, and failures. In this chapter, I will present an overview of what I consider the three major trends to promote character education as they relate to the coding playground: the narrative, the reasoning, and the experiential approaches.

After describing these three, I present how my approach integrates elements of all of them by using the learning of computer programming as a tool to promote positive behaviors and character development. As children in the coding playground learn to create and share their own computational projects, they explore and practice the ten values in the palette of virtues. They might also add new values and mix and match existing ones. CAL proposes an intentional awareness of the values at play when learning to code. Since the palette of virtues is dynamic, it invites educators to incorporate their own colors and to extend and adapt to the needs and cultural practices of their own classrooms.

The Narrative Approach: Moral Identities

Narrative plays an important role in the construction of identity. We tell and listen to stories. We make sense of the world. Some of these stories represent different fragments of our experience. Over time, we develop a life narrative that revisits our moral choices and invites us to think about consequences for ourselves and others. Slowly, through those narratives, we construct a moral identity. We become aware of our character strengths.

Narratives operate at three different levels: cognitive, social, and emotional. At the cognitive level, narratives are fundamental constituents of human memory. They provide a distinctive way of creating, ordering, and understanding an experience. At the social level, the tales that one knows can define the social group or culture to which one belongs. Myths, legends, and traditional stories provide a sense of continuity between generations as well as models for human behavior that define a particular group. Finally, at the emotional level, narratives allow us to work and rework our feelings about past experiences. As Anna Freud and the growing field of narrative therapy have shown, through verbal play or the written experience of storytelling, people can find not only recreation but also self-cure.

Narratives appeal to the intellect and the emotional lives; they invite imagination and anchor us to traditions. It is not surprising, then, that narratives are highly used to teach and learn about values and to promote character strengths and moral development. Within the narrative approach, several programs have flourished and perished over time to teach about values. For example, the "Bag of Virtues," exemplified by William Bennett's *Book of Virtues*, involves a compendium of children's stories that present universal human values. Fairy tales, myths, and biographies are also commonly used. Different cultural, ethnical and religious groups have their own repertoire that can serve pedagogical functions.

The assumption of the narrative approach to moral education is that an external authority (the writer, teacher, curricula, institution, community, religion, culture, country, etc.) selects the moral truths to be told through stories. Children listen to the narratives and eventually appropriate them by internalizing the conveyed values. This might or might not work, depending on the quality of the experience, but always requires a shared agreement about cherished values and character strengths.

For example, in religious settings, the teacher might use biblical stories. The hope is that by telling and retelling stories, moral codes and ethical insights will be passed from generation to generation. In creative learning environments, stories are adapted and reinterpreted so that children can identify with plot and characters in the context of their own lives. Some believe that only chaos and disorder can result from multiple interpretations and advocate for literal readings of foundational religious narratives. Fundamentalists are the most extreme cases, and a narrow interpretation of the story coupled with the certainty of holding a moral truth can lead to indoctrination instead of education. However, when interpretation is welcomed, the narrative approach can lead to the development of moral identities within a group that shares beliefs and practices, a history, and a vision of the future.

The narrative approach only works if people agree on the virtues conveyed through the stories. What happens when virtues are not shared by everyone? Are there credible universal narratives that can bring about global ethics and global character strengths? These questions are difficult to answer in pluralistic societies. Thus, a different approach, one that engages moral reasoning as opposed to the content of the stories, is also appealing.

The Reasoning Approach: Moral Thought

Extending Piaget's work on children's moral judgment, American psychologist Lawrence Kohlberg identified six stages of moral development. These start with value judgments of a highly egocentric form, "what I like is what is good," and are followed by a decentering process, "something is good because it is good for somebody else." The final stage is reached when abstract moral principles develop, such as "I don't kill because killing is bad."

In their research, Kohlberg and his colleagues used fictional dilemmas to categorize and assess stages of moral development. The assumption behind this cognitive developmental approach is that there is a universal progression from a concrete to an abstract way of thinking about moral issues. Although the universal stages have been challenged in regard to cross-cultural and gender validity, Kohlberg's work was instrumental in creating a new field within psychology: moral development.

When Kohlberg's stages of moral development were taken into the classroom, they were translated into the practice of engaging students in discussions of hypothetical dilemmas and emulated the Socratic method of inquiry. However, these philosophical debates rarely lead to behavioral changes. In the later years of his life, Kohlberg realized the importance of students' involvement in social institutions to promote change. He urged educators to transform their schools into "just communities" to accelerate students' stages of moral development. These participatory democracies could serve as a model of the larger political community in which the child would participate as an adult. Kohlberg's "just community" approach was successfully implemented and studied in schools and prisons. Today, his legacy is alive in internal school committees and the model of "schools within schools" that have some level of operational power and autonomy.

The cognitive approach to moral development is attractive to educators. On the one hand, it provides an intellectual bridge between the moral and the civic domains. On the other hand, it can be implemented in most educational institutions. Born as a reaction to the perceived danger of indoctrination carried by the narrative approach, it values the process of moral reasoning but not its content. For example, programs such as values clarification, originally espoused by Louis Raths and colleagues in the mid-60s, helps children understand that the process of valuing is present in every situation in which we need to make a decision: capital punishment, abortion, relationships, or choosing a book or gift for someone. This perspective helps the individual clarify, express, and organize her values while rejecting the set of values imposed by external authority. The teacher orchestrates the learning situation to help students express their own feelings and apply valuation skills. The assumption is that students need practice choosing among moral alternatives and teachers can facilitate the clarification process rather than indoctrinate.

The values clarification approach is built upon the implicit assumption that the process of valuation has little relationship to historical, religious, social, or familial contexts. The student is encouraged to clarify her personal values without exploring how those relate to her identity. Critiques of this approach claim that regarding values as matters of personal concern and choice carries the danger of naïve relativism. While currently few educators confidently advocate for the values clarification approach, teacher neutrality and hesitance to actively address ethical issues in the classroom might originate in this perspective.

Over the years, other programs were developed along the lines of moral reasoning. For example, ethical inquiry by Lipman teaches students how to use logic to distinguish better from worse reasoning. The teacher and the school are models of behavior and responsible citizenship, and thus the method of teaching needs to be consistent with what is taught. Lipman's ethical inquiry and Kohlberg's just community share the emphasis on disciplined discussion and community of inquiry as conditions for moral education. The individual is not necessarily encouraged to explore her own personal values, as in values clarification, but to cultivate civic values and apply critical thinking.

While engaging children in reasoning and critical thinking might avoid indoctrination, thinking does not always lead to doing. Thinking about a moral, good life is not the same as living a moral, good life.

The Experiential Approach: A Moral Life

The idea that education emerges from experience, and vice versa, dates back to John Dewey's experiential learning philosophy. For this prominent American scholar from the first half of the twentieth century, education must include a civic and moral imperative. Back in the early 1900s, Dewey understood schools as social centers to promote democratic living and behavior and to influence cooperative membership in the community. While in its early forms, membership to the community was understood as local community; after the First World War, progressives rallied around the idea of expanding civic education programs to the world community. Today, service learning, community service, and volunteering programs make experiential learning across the globe a reality in the modern educational system.

These popular opportunities provide students with guidance, mentorship, and practice at being moral actors. They combine academic learning with personally meaningful encounters. Starting in kindergarten, children are given small chores such as feeding the classroom's pet or straightening the desks and chairs. As they grow, they can tutor younger students and eventually work up to more demanding service activities such as leading clubs, organizing fundraisers, volunteering at shelters, and generally contributing to the greater good.

As students go to college, an array of opportunities expands from gap years devoted to local and international community service to service-learning trips during school breaks. Alternative experiences and trips focus on a wide range of issues such as poverty, education, refugee resettlement, disaster relief, and clean water. Students can choose the experience based on their own interests. They might travel with a professor to a site for an intensive weeklong experience, or they might join an already existing organization. Service-learning trips during school breaks, originated in the 1980s as a counter to traditional spring breaks, is a growing trend that now even offers credit.

Service-learning experiences are one of the many ways in which students can learn to engage in civic life through activism. Research shows that adults are more likely to vote and participate in civic life if, as youth, they were involved in community-based extracurricular activities and civic education programs. Thus, the importance of these kinds of experiences promotes not only character development but also civic engagement. The experiential approach speaks directly to the formation of a good citizen and attracts a wide network of supporters.

These kinds of experiences position multicultural understanding as a bedrock of American democracy. However, a critical perspective illuminates how, using the language of economic prosperity and civic education, the globalization of the Western mindset, hegemonic policies, and power structures are legitimized.

The Values in Coding as Another Language

CAL incorporates elements from these three approaches to moral education: the narrative, the reasoning, and the experiential. First, inspired by the narrative approach, children engage in a coding playground in which they tell and listen to stories and share orally and in written form their own learning process. Second, grounded on the reasoning approach, children develop logical and abstract thinking while programming and debugging their projects and translating their ideas into an algorithm. Third, influenced by the experiential approach, children make computational projects to share with others and participate in a learning community in which a palette of virtues guides curricular decisions and classroom experiences. In the process, values are explored and practiced. While the coding playground reinforces ten values in the palette of virtues, new values can be added.

The narrative approach, and its focus on telling stories to construct moral identities, is present every time children are asked to think about themselves as agents of their own learning. Children who learn to code become producers of technologically rich projects as opposed to consumers. They develop an identity as creators. When in the coding playground, these children are invited to reflect about their own creations and the design process they followed, presenting an opportunity to tell their stories. The stories they tell can focus on the "I–It" relationship with the technology, to borrow Martin Buber's language, or can include the "I–Thou" bond with others. A teacher following the CAL curriculum will find herself inviting children to think about the latter and not only the former. For example, she will ask about how children worked together in teams, how they helped each other, and how they showed gratitude to each other.

The reasoning approach, and its goal to promote logical thinking and problem-solving skills, is inherent in the activity of coding.

Programming is about creating a sequence of logical instructions, being able to think in abstract ways, and translating those instructions into a symbolic system of representation that the computer can understand: a programming language. While programmers have been around for a century, philosophers have existed long before, thinking about how to translate human language into a structured argument with consistent logic in its premises and conclusions. Much of the work of critical thinking in philosophy involves mastering structured language to translate the messiness and vagueness of human language. The CAL approach, by focusing on learning to code as learning another language, embraces this. Coding is a way to organize our thinking and uses a symbolic system to express it. As an heir to Aristotle's logical systems, programming can be a gateway to critical thinking about not only technical problems but also societal issues.

Today, more than ever, we need a critical mindset. The rapid acceleration of new discoveries and technical innovations, coupled with the unparalleled access to information "anytime, anywhere" through the internet, and the use of artificial intelligence and machine learning, has created new sets of problems. The basic intellectual tools to think about these problems has been around since the days of Socrates and Aristotle: understanding the structure of an argument and translating human language into the premises and conclusions that make up the basis for logical analysis. These intellectual tools allow us to judge information, to evaluate evidence, and to make decisions applying formal rules. However, the intellectual toolbox needs to be expanded. Coding adds the ability to create new realities through novel systems and processes.

Although most grade schools do not teach formal logic, its practical application in the form of structured thinking through an artificial language, that is, computer programming, is being learned by more students today than ever before. If we limit its application to the growth of a STEM workforce, we will be missing the great opportunity envisioned by the early philosophers of ancient Greece: to form the ethical character of future citizens who can grow as autonomous individuals capable of thinking systematically and independently, problem-solve when needed, and act toward the good of self and society.

The experiential approach is found everywhere in the coding playground. Children learn by doing, experimenting, trial and error, collaborating with others and solving social conflicts, feeling overwhelmed with the challenge ahead, and learning how to manage time and frustration. In the social interactions of the coding playground, character strengths are developed and values are put to practice. The six Cs or behaviors of the PTD framework (content creation, creativity, choices of conduct, communication, collaboration, and community building) are intentionally promoted in the CAL coding experience.

Most specifically, several pedagogical tools explicitly use narrative, reasoning, and experiential learning:

- **Book integration:** The curriculum is designed around stories. While it is key for these stories to have a sequence of events that can be retold, the content might vary. Teachers are encouraged to find their own stories and adapt lessons to them. Stories are not chosen because of their moral message or the values they promote but because of their "algorithmic" rhythm: the sequencing of orderly events that engage thinking about cause and effect. Most of the final coding projects involve children retelling and changing the end of the story. A CAL-trained teacher will know what books to choose, and will engage children in thinking about choices of conduct by playing around with different endings. She will be aware of the palette of virtues and bring it up as it fits. In addition, she will encourage conversation about responsibilities and consequences and the moral and ethical implications of certain choices.

- **Technology circles:** Most early childhood classrooms have a central space, usually around a rug, in which children come together in a circle to greeting each other, singing, going over the daily schedule, or reading a story. Circle time provides protected time in a consistent fashion for listening, developing attention span, promoting oral communication, and learning new concepts and skills. The curriculum builds on this practice and intentionally sets up technology circles at the beginning and end of the day. These provide scaffolded opportunities for children to talk with each other about their coding projects, the challenges and solutions explored, the strategies discovered, and the feelings encountered. The use of oral language in the technology circles addresses not only literacy standards but also the nurturing of human relationships. Children are taught how to provide constructive feedback and engage in peer-interviews. When the Cs of communication and collaboration are practiced, a teacher trained in the CAL pedagogy will ask questions so that children can share both their technical expertise and aspects of their identity: How did you feel while working on this? What did you learn about yourself as a learner? How did this experience help you get to know yourself and others better? During the technology circles, the palette of virtues becomes alive through the children's personal reflections.

- **Design journals:** Every child is given a notebook to keep track of ideas and sketches, to brainstorm about her project, and to document progress. While younger children might record or draw, older ones are encouraged to write. Depending on the grade level, the journal writing is structured to meet different literacy frameworks. Design journals are authentic tools used in many sectors and industries. For example, in engineering, they serve not only for planning but also as a legal record in case of a legal proceeding. In the coding classroom, the journals serve as a learning record for assessment and for reflective practice.

The classroom practice of keeping design journals during the creation process makes transparent to the children (as well as teachers and parents) their own thinking, their own learning trajectories, and the project's evolution over time. In addition, design journals serve for practicing with the symbolic system of human languages.

- **Community open house:** Children work toward creating a final integrative project to share with others during a final open house. Open houses provide authentic opportunities for children to share and celebrate the learning process and product with others who are also invested in their learning. During these open houses, family, friends, and community members visit the class for a demonstration. Creativity is displayed in the use of novel arts and crafts materials as well as the choice of programming blocks and settings. The goal of demonstrating a project is to foster computational thinking and technological fluency among not only the participating children and teachers but also the wider community. It is an opportunity to extend the I–Thou encounters outside of the classroom. Each child is given the chance to play the role of teacher as she explains how she built, programmed, and worked through problems. While the technological accomplishments are celebrated, it is the story children can tell around the project that counts most. It is in the child's narration that we can observe if and how the palette of virtues has been explored. A CAL-trained teacher will encourage children to discuss how they needed patience, perseverance, open-mindedness, and optimism to work on their projects and will invite children to express their gratitude to all of those who helped them in the process.

- **Collaboration web:** This low-tech pedagogical tool is designed to help children become aware of their collaborative patterns in the coding playground. Along with design journals and robotic kits or tablets, children are given personalized printouts with their photograph in the center of the page. Their photographs are displayed along with those of all other children in the class, arranged in a circle surrounding their own photo. This represents their classroom community and intentionally shows children that learning does not happen alone. In preparation for the final open house, children are invited to think about those individuals who helped them and those whom they helped in the process of creating their projects. Children are asked to draw arrows in their collaboration webs in two different directions: from their own picture to the pictures of children who they helped and from the picture of classmates who helped them to their own picture. For this purpose, collaboration is defined as getting or giving help with a project, programming or working together on a common task, and lending or borrowing materials. Teachers collect the collaboration webs and discuss them during technology circles. They can graph the data with children and observe patterns.

- **Gratitude cards:** Using the "data" provided by the collaboration webs, children are encouraged to write, or draw, thank-you notes to the classmates and adults who helped them the most. In contrast to polite thank-you cards, the writing of gratitude cards is an exercise in self-reflection and perspective-taking. It is an acknowledgment of the importance of developing and practicing values and not only technical skills. Some teachers choose to hand out these gratitude cards during the final open house in a public ceremony, while others do it in the intimacy of the classroom routine.

- **Expertise badges:** Differentiation of roles is important to the growth of a responsible learning community. Teachers can assign children expertise badges that carry the responsibility of helping others on a topic for which the child is an expert. Some badges might be technical, such as efficient scanner or expert with nested loops, some might be social such as conflict mediator, and others emotional, such as stress reliever. As the curriculum progresses, children master different areas. A trained teacher will encourage the child to try on new roles and wear different expertise badges at different times. The focus on learning to code is as important as helping children become flexible in their approach and develop an inner compass to guide their actions in a just and responsible way.

- **Diversity of materials:** The coding playground provides both high-tech materials, such as robots and tablets, and low-tech materials, such as arts and crafts, and recyclables to support creative expression, graphic organizers to sequence activities, and anchor charts for reinforcing concepts. In addition, there are posters with the design process, the six Cs of PTD, and the palette of virtues. There are large, printed icons of the different blocks of the programming language so that children can play with those and incorporate them into unplugged games such as "Programmer Says." This game mimics the traditional "Simon Says," in which children need to pay attention to distinguish which actions told by Simon (or the programmer) to perform or not. Teachers make important choices in the way they display and introduce the diversity of materials to the children. The kind of storage and access can change the way children experience the coding playground. For example, when working with robots, some teachers may choose to give a complete robotic kit to each group of students. Children may label the kit with their names and use the same kit for the duration of the curriculum. Other teachers may choose to take apart the kits, have materials sorted by type, and place all the materials in a central location for children to collect. If working with tablets, it is important to remind children that tablets need to be charged. Some schools provide carts that roll the tablets into the classroom, and therefore children and teachers do not need to worry about batteries running out. Other classrooms have their own equipment, and it is therefore the classroom's responsibility to have everything ready to use. Regardless of the technological platform, the curriculum reminds teachers of the importance of setting expectations for how materials will be used and taken care of. This is an opportunity to explore the responsibility associated with creation and the associated values in the palette of virtues.

- **Music and movement:** The curriculum positions programming as an expressive language. Therefore, it welcomes the use of other expressive languages, such as music and dance. After all, those also have symbolic systems of representation that one can get to master if time is devoted to practicing them. CAL includes catchy songs, such as the design process song, the robot parts song, and the clean-up song to the tune of popular children's songs. In addition, several games that use movement such as robot corners and freeze dance are integrated. One of my favorites is an activity that invites children to program their robot or ScratchJr kitten to dance the Hokey Pokey, which provides a structured sequence of actions, and children can dance along.

A Window into Their World: The Best Use of Her Time

Nancy entered the classroom smiling, sat down on her spot on the technology circle, and waited for class to begin. Ms. Cleary welcomed everyone back from recess and invited her kindergarten students to sing the robot part song. Nancy stood up, delighted, and danced along moving side to side: "The body is connected to the motor, the motor is connected to the wheel, so move robot, move."

After singing, the children discussed different robots they had seen and compared them to KIBO. They also shared how excited they were to finally get to play with KIBO today. They could not wait for Ms. Cleary to end the technology circle. Finally, Ms. Cleary invited everyone to get up and walk over to the small tables in the back of the room. She had organized and sorted all of the KIBO materials into different storage bins. There were bins with wheels and motors and sound sensors and programming blocks with different color stickers. Ms. Cleary split her students into pairs. She asked each pair to approach the tables and collect their robotic materials from the bins. She gave each pair an empty tray and explained, "To start with, every pair needs to get a KIBO body, motors, wheels and at least three programming blocks."

Nancy and her partner waited patiently as students mulled over the KIBO bins. Finally, it was their turn. They searched the bins and took as many parts as they could fit on their tray. Soon, they found a quiet place on the room and began building. They worked collaboratively, taking turns. They put a wheel and a motor on each side of the KIBO robot and set aside the other four they had collected. They created a program with three blocks, as Ms. Cleary requested, using a green block to start, a blue block to shake, and a red block to end. They left aside three other red blocks they had collected.

Excited, the children started to program KIBO to shake. They did not get discouraged when the scanning did not work. They did not call their teacher over. They worked together and kept trying. As they explored different strategies for scanning, they heard Ms. Cleary clap three times. That was the signal for everyone to stop doing what they were doing and listen carefully. "How many wheels and how many motors does KIBO need to move forward?" asked Ms. Cleary to the class. "Two," responded the group in unison. Some children lifted the motors up, others shouted the number two, and a few used their index fingers to show the number two. "Exactly, only two," smiled Ms. Cleary. "Now, please look at your trays and the floor around you. I suspect many of you will find that you took more than two motors and wheels. We have a problem. Some of you were not able to grab any of them because when time came to find them in the bins, they were all gone."

The children giggled uncomfortably. Slowly, most of them started to return the overflow materials to the bins in the back of the room. This teaching moment, from the time Mrs. Cleary invited them to choose what they needed to put on their trays to the time she asked them to return what they did not need, took approximately ten minutes. For a class that generally lasts forty-five minutes, that is a very long time. However, it was one of the best uses of her time, an opportunity to practice some of the values in the palette of virtues.

Ms. Cleary had planned for this to happened. She expected children would take as many motors and wheels as possible, and she was aware that some pairs were going to be left with nothing to work with until she called the class to return what they would not need. She was cognizant that she risked some children getting upset for a little bit. She also knew this was an authentic opportunity to experience the importance of sharing, of taking what is needed and not more.

Ms. Cleary was trained on the CAL-KIBO curriculum and therefore knew that it did not matter how fast the robots were built and programmed as much as the process of doing it. In her kindergarten coding playground, character strengths were as valued as technical efficiency. The time she took to engage the class in a discussion about fairness and generosity, not by preaching or telling a story but by having her students experience the lack of, was the best use of her time. She knew that children would eventually learn how to program KIBO. However, learning about values in an authentic way and putting them to use required constant practice.

7

The Palette of Virtues

Ari (five years old): Give me the ear!

Cala (five years old): It is mine.

Ari: But there are a lot of them in the sensor box.

Cala: Yes, but I found this one and it is mine.

Ari: Can you go find another one for me?

Cala: Sure!

Approximately once a month, five women gather in one of our homes to study. We are two academics: me and a neuroscientist, a psychologist, a librarian, and an engineer trained as a physicist. At one time, there was also a lawyer, who became a rabbi. We study Musar, a Jewish spiritual practice to live a meaningful and ethical life. We read Jewish texts and discuss them. We explore how this ancient tradition can bring about personal transformation through a Jewish lens.

While we drink tea and share fruits and cookies, we immerse ourselves in a shared inner journey. Musar offers a curriculum of ethical qualities spanning forty-eight universal *midot* (Hebrew plural of *mida*, character strength, value, or virtue) like kindness, humility, and joy. We start by reading a text from the Torah (Old Testament) and then dive into selected scholarly interpretations. Finally, we move on to discuss how a chosen *mida* plays out in the text and how it relates to our personal lives. Sometimes we laugh, and other times we cry. Before going home, we agree on "homework" or a monthly *mida* practice until the next meeting.

Musar is a field of study and an individual practice anchored in the Jewish tradition concerned with ethical instruction, practical wisdom, and guidance. For centuries, the Musar masters recognized that simply learning about values does not translate into action. Studying kindness does not make us more kind. There is a need for practice and experience. Musar was considered a minor part of the Jewish literature until the nineteenth century, when Rabbi Israel Salanter created the Musar movement that transformed an individual experience into a community practice. By 1939, Musar had a significant presence in the major *yeshivas* (house of studies) in Eastern Europe. Tragically, many teachers and practitioners were murdered in the Holocaust.

Today, Musar has become widely practiced in the liberal Jewish world, beyond the Orthodox community. People are attracted to its mindfulness and ethical aspects. Different teachers have their own methods. For example, some daily practices include a morning mantra, a mindful action as one goes through the day, and nightly journaling. In our group, we incorporated a monthly phone call as a "check in" to address challenges when practicing the *mida* of the month.

What does this old tradition have to do with new technologies? Why am I describing Musar in a book about coding? What are the connections between the ancient practices of a spiritual journey and the new habits of a cognitive adventure? The coding playground provides an intentional opportunity to practice *midot* and to develop virtues. CAL is not only a pedagogy for learning computer science but also for acquiring, promoting, and reflecting on character strengths.

Stanford professor Carol Dweck coined the term *growth mindset* to refer to the belief that talents or skills can be developed through hard work, good strategies, and input from others. My work shows that coding can lead to a growth mindset. However, it also offers an opportunity to develop a growth spirit. This is the confidence that we can become better human beings. While a growth mindset highlights intellectual talents and abilities, a growth spirit also includes emotional, ethical, and character strengths.

Sherry Turkle wrote extensively about how the computer's true potential was its "second self" nature. Computers are not only instrumental tools but also psychological machines that serve us to think about identity and about what makes us uniquely human. She eloquently explained that this is not because the computer has a psychology of its own but because it provokes us to think about our own psychological and social lives. It can impact our awareness of ourselves, of one another, and of our relationships with the world.

My first conversation with Turkle happened in Spanish in 1987, sitting in my bedroom in Buenos Aires, Argentina, when I was seventeen years old. It was not exactly a two-way interactive dialogue; it was more like me writing in the margins of her newly translated book, *The Second Self: Computers and the Human Spirit*. Although I was still in high school, I read and reread those pages many times. I engaged deeply with the idea that computers could help us explore our own identities, that they could become a second self. Little did I know that a decade later I would have weekly conversations with Turkle in her MIT office or at her house in Boston when she became a thesis committee member for my doctoral work at the MIT Media Lab.

In this book I am building on Turkle's ideas. Technology is powerful when it can engage people in self-reflection, community building, and meaningful conversations. These are the kind of I–Thou encounters that Martin Buber refers to. I learned from Turkle to understand technology as a window into the human spirit. However, I am not fascinated by the computer per se but by our relationship to it. When we code, we create with and through the computer. We learn its language and can enter its world to make our world a better place. We express ourselves: we become intentional agents who can creatively produce unique projects.

The Coding Playground

In 2012 I published my second book, *Designing Digital Experiences for Positive Youth Development: From Playpen to Playground*. Most people loved the metaphor of playgrounds versus playpens to understand the role that new technologies can have in children's lives. Playgrounds are open-ended. Playpens are limited. Playgrounds invite fantasy play, imagination and creativity, social interaction, and teamwork; there are spaces to experiment with conflict resolution, and they require less adult supervision. In contrast to the open-ended playground, playpens convey lack of freedom to experiment, lack of autonomy for exploration, lack of creative opportunities, and lack of taking risks. Although playpens are safer, playgrounds offer infinite possibilities for growth and learning. Tools such as ScratchJr and KIBO are coding playgrounds for young children.

The playground versus playpen metaphor was successful. However, it eclipsed some of the important ideas behind it. Theoretical frameworks are not as popular as metaphors. In the book I described the PTD framework that I developed. It consists of six behaviors or activities, the six Cs, that we can often see at the neighborhood playground and we want to promote in the coding playground: content creation, creativity, choices of conduct, communication, collaboration, and community building. Inspired by the field of positive youth development and my colleague Richard Lerner, I coined the phrase "positive technological development" to describe

content
creation

creativity

choice of
conduct

communication

collaboration

community
building

Figure 7.1
The six Cs of the PTD framework

a theoretical lens that captures these psychosocial behaviors in the context of using technology. I take an interventionist approach. PTD provides guidelines for designing and evaluating technological programs to promote character strengths through positive behaviors or activities. Below, I describe the six behaviors, or six Cs, of PTD that can be found in the best coding playgrounds (figure 7.1).

- **Content creation:** The activity of coding involves using an artificial language to create. In this journey, the child engages in a series of interrelated steps that might or might not be linear: the design process. To create her own project, she learns to ask questions, identify a goal, formulate an action plan, make an initial attempt, test, evaluate, and revise her ideas by assessing what went wrong and what could be done better. At the end of the creation process, she has a sharable project.

- **Creativity:** Coding playgrounds are playful spaces in which creativity can flourish. The ability to transcend traditional strategies to imagine and create original projects supports personally meaningful expression. A creative child can frame problems in innovative ways and find divergent approaches and solutions.

However, creativity requires training and hard work. Contradicting some popular myths, the creative child is not necessarily the one who wakes up one morning saying "Eureka!" but the one who is disciplined in her work, takes risks, and can find new connections.

- **Choices of conduct:** Anytime we do something, we make choices and must assume consequences. This process, when authentic, builds character. On the one hand, our character strengths inform the choices we make. On the other hand, those choices have an impact on our character. We are surrounded by news about people choosing to use their coding skills in positive or negative ways, to help or to harm society. Coding is a tool and, like any other tool, can be used for good or bad. Like a hammer, it can build or destroy. The coding playground engages children in situations in which they will have to make choices and provides a palette of virtues so that those choices can be made with a sense of purpose and responsibility.

- **Communication:** In the playground, there is conversation. Language socialization plays a key role in cognitive development as well as personal, social, and emotional growth. A healthy playground is not a quiet place. Similarly, in the coding playground children talk to externalize and exchange ideas and thoughts. However, most programming languages do not have a built-in feature to promote communication. A good curriculum provides explicit communication mechanisms and strategies to support the formation and sustainment of positive bonds through coding. It is only through dialogue that I–Thou encounters can happen.

- **Collaboration:** Two or more people working on a team is not the same as collaboration. For collaboration to happen, there is a need for a shared goal and cooperation on a common task. This can be challenging in early childhood; for a typically developing young child, the turn-taking, self-control, and self-regulation required to effectively collaborate on a project is difficult. Coding provides another opportunity to practice these skills because teamwork is intentionally built into the curriculum.

- **Community building:** The previously discussed Cs of communication and collaboration support the establishment and sustainment of social relationships in the coding playground. Community building takes this a step further by offering mechanisms for giving back to others and contributing to our communities. For example, open houses and family coding nights in which children demo their coding projects are an authentic opportunity to share and celebrate the processes and products of learning with parents, family, and friends.

Although in my previous work I described these six Cs as "positive behaviors," I realize that what makes them positive, or not, is the intentionality behind them: the values or character strengths that inform and are expressed through these behaviors. The six Cs are value neutral. We can create a video game to practice shooting skills or to learn the ABCs, we can communicate in dysfunctional ways to harm others or to praise, or we can choose to include others in our teams or exclude them. A coding playground needs guiding values and not only behaviors. While different cultural contexts might have a diversity of values, the activity of programming in a culture in which the act of creative production is rewarded lends itself to values such as curiosity, determination, and persistence.

The Ten Virtues

What are the values of the people who use technology to produce as opposed to merely consume? How are these values expressed through actions? How do we teach values in the coding playground?

Are these values universal or particular? These are difficult questions to answer. Over the centuries, attempts have been made to create lists and classifications of universal values. The challenges are many, starting with the difficulty of a shared vocabulary.

I am standing on the shoulders of positive psychologists, moral philosophers, and religious thinkers who created lists and categorized them. However, I am thinking as an educational designer, as someone who uses the language of code to create, to express, and to communicate. I am inspired by artists. The artist creates a color palette rather than a list to work with. In this book, based on over two-and-a-half decades of working with children and teachers, I offer my palette of virtues for the coding playground. I am not advocating a hierarchy in the importance of the values, nor I am claiming that these are the only values in the color wheel. I am not concerned with primary, secondary, or tertiary colors or values, nor am I advancing a theoretical contribution to the study of ethics and moral philosophy in education.

I am proposing a metaphor to think about values in the coding playground. The artist chooses colors and creates her own palette. She mixes and matches, and she adds new colors and continues to mix. A little bit here, a little bit there. She creates shades and saturations. She finds harmony and dissonance. She uses her imagination and there is no absolute right and wrong; it depends on the context of how the colors are used and their relationships. Ultimately, it is about intentionality.

The metaphor of the color palette is in sharp contrast with the popular paint by number kits. These kits, which have been around since the 1950s, present a board with a drawing divided into different areas to paint. Each area has a number marking and a corresponding numbered paint to use. The kits come with little compartmentalized boxes where the numbered colors are stored. The artist's job is to match numbered paint areas to numbered paint colors, making sure there is no spilling over. She is encouraged to wash the paintbrush every time a new numbered color is being used so that the original drawing can be exactly replicated.

While the color palette invites messiness and choices, the paint by number kits provide structure and directions. As metaphors for thinking about the role of values in education, they convey very different messages. In the coding playground, the CAL approach offers a palette of virtues as opposed to a paint by virtues kit. As the artist develops her color palette, she needs to explore, get it wrong, and try again. The paint by numbers kit is safer. We do what we are told. If we are careful and develop the skill, the likelihood of success is very high. We do not need to think about context, consequences, and responsible choices. The boundaries are given to us, and our job is to follow the guidelines at the cost of limited individual expression and creativity.

Color palettes and paint by number kits are metaphors. They evoke strategies for helping children develop personal and ethical values, character strengths, and positive behaviors. As educators, we know that teaching a class in which children can experiment with their own color palettes is harder, but it is also more rewarding. We can see the engagement, excitement, and frustration. Each child is following her inner compass but at the same time must adhere to some universals. The best learning happens when children can experience color theory, when they discover how humans perceive color and the visual effects of how colors mix, match, or contrast with each other, not when we instruct them how to do it. It is similar with values.

While many classrooms have a list of their school's core values or virtues hanging on the walls, it is doubtful that children will appropriate them if they do not experience them. Of course, experimenting with values is riskier than experimenting with colors. There are people and relationships involved, not only aesthetics. The coding playground can become a safe place to experiment with values. However, there are universals that must be accepted, for example, the golden rule that says we must treat others as we would like them to treat us.

There are also universals when working with color palettes. There are physics, wavelength, and the wiring of the brain. Back in 1666, Sir Isaac Newton designed the first color wheel based on his scientific investigations with prisms, mirrors, and light. Artists and designers still use it to make their own color palettes. Some artists develop a unique identity by only working with a specific color palette, and others work with multiple palettes. The color palette is both unique and universal.

Color palettes are dynamic. The painter arranges and mixes different paints for each of her creations. Likewise, in the values palette, an educator can intentionally choose the values to put into practice in her lessons and incorporate new values as needed. In the palette of virtues I put together for the coding playground, I work with ten values: curiosity, open-mindedness, perseverance, patience, optimism, honesty, fairness, generosity, gratitude, and forgiveness (figure 7.2). However, others can include their own values and make substitutions.

Mitch Resnick uses the imagery of the paintbrush for describing the activity of coding. In 2006, he wrote that "in my view, computers will not live up to their potential until we start to think of them less like televisions and more like paintbrushes." Resnick was referring to the creative expressive potential of paintbrushes. I am extending the metaphor. The paintbrush by itself is not enough; it needs colors. The artist chooses the colors. She is aware of her choices and understands that context and relationships play a big role. She has intentionality.

In the coding playground, the child is the artist who learns to code, and the paintbrush is the programming language that supports creativity. The colors are the values the child learns and expresses while coding. The coding playground becomes an art

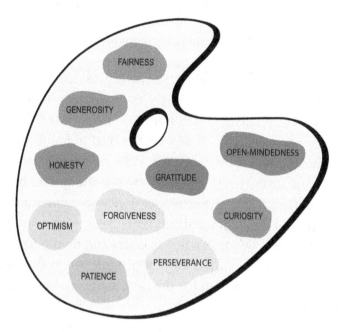

Figure 7.2
The palette of virtues

studio for practicing a palette of virtues. Creative programming can be a pathway for character development.

The following vignettes are examples of how the ten values in the palette of virtues play out in the coding playground. They tell stories as opposed to providing academic definitions. As you read through them, pay attention to the teacher's role. You will see that in most situations, the teachers, who were trained in the CAL pedagogy, had to choose what to prioritize in the short time they were allocated to work with coding in the classroom. In some specific cases, they had to choose between advancing students' technical skills or character strengths. They chose the latter. In the coding playground, socioemotional development does not take the back seat; good teachers plan their lessons, but great teachers know how to slow down if the opportunity to work with values arises.

Curiosity

Noun: a strong desire to know or learn something; novelty seeking

Tyla waits in line to get her tablet. She is very excited. Her first-grade teacher, Ms. Robins, said that today they would make their very own story with ScratchJr. Tyla's mind has been racing with ideas. As she eagerly walks to her seat with her iPad in hand, she knows she will make a story about penguins. They are her favorite animals. Although she loves them, she does not like the boring black and white color of their bodies. She wishes they were more colorful.

She opens her design journal and starts sketching a rainbow penguin with crayons. She tries a few sketches and then puts the journal down. She wonders what kind of penguin she is drawing. She launches a Google search on her iPad and starts browsing images of penguins from all over the world and chooses the Galapagos penguin as inspiration. While she is drawing, Ms. Robins tells everyone that it is time to put away their design journals and open ScratchJr.

Ms. Robins explains how to get to the app's character creation tool so that the children can make their own characters for their stories. On Tyla's screen shines a bright canvas underlined by an array of colors, ScratchJr's paint tools. Tyla wants to use these tools to make a ScratchJr rainbow penguin, like the one she drew on her journal. She taps a bright pink color and begins to draw the outline of her character. As she works, the rainbow penguin becomes a pink penguin with long purple hair and a red cape around its neck. She loves the way it looks so far, but the body looks much blander than it did on her design journal. She thinks for a moment and adds blue polka dots. Tyla smiles. She likes it much better.

Noticing that Tyla has stopped using the iPad, Ms. Robins walks over to her and asks, "Are you all done designing your character, Tyla?" Tyla nods energetically, saying "Look, Ms. Robins! I figured out how to give my pink penguin polka dots!" She points to the teal circles that dot her penguin's body. Ms. Robins replies, "That's great,

Tyla! Since you're already done making your penguin, do you want to start programming her?" Tyla nods. "What is your story about?" asks Ms. Robins. Tyla is not sure. She has only thought about the main character, not what role the character would play in the story. "No problem," says Ms. Robins. "We have not discussed the story yet in class. We will. But not today. The other kids are still making their characters. Why don't you start exploring ScratchJr programming blocks on your own? Why don't you try some of them and see what you can discover?"

Tyla's eyes grow big and round. "I will be like a ScratchJr detective!" she exclaims, turning to her iPad. She decides to try with the purple blocks first by dragging a random one into her program. When she presses the green flag to run it, she watches as her penguin vanishes before her eyes. "Woah!" Tyla jumps and says, "I figured out how to make my penguin disappear!" She makes the penguin appear and vanish again. "This is going to be a magic penguin now," she announces. As she tests out the other purple blocks, she creates a penguin that can appear and reappear, grow to the size of a skyscraper, and shrink to the size of an ant.

Now that she made a magic penguin, she decides to go back to the character creation tool and edit her drawing. She makes a magician's hat and a magic wand for her penguin. As she begins to explore the orange blocks, Ms. Robins calls out that it is time to put the tablets away and go to recess. "Aw, man," Tyla mutters, looking at her unfinished work. As she lines up to put her tablet back on the charging station, she knows that her penguin was saved and will still be in her ScratchJr project tomorrow.

In Ms. Robins's coding playground, curiosity plays an important role. It inspires children to create their own meaningful projects, to learn new programming concepts and tools, and to explore different resources. Ms. Robins knows that she often evokes curiosity in her virtues palette. As she teaches, she asks questions, explores ideas, and tries things out. She wants to model a curious attitude.

Ms. Robins understands that as a teacher, she has the responsibility to not only talk about values but to also display them through her own actions. She sees her job as a keeper of curiosity. That is not difficult since first graders are always curious. However, she knows some children will lose their curiosity as they move along the educational system. She hopes her coding playground will help maintain their inquisitive stance.

Open-mindedness

Noun: the quality of being willing to consider ideas, opinions, and feelings that are new or different from your own; flexibility in taking different perspectives

During ScratchJr time, Sumant learns how to use the send message block. "As soon as a character has the send message block," his first-grade teacher explains, "it tells another character to start doing something else." She points to the screen projector displaying an icon with an envelope. "See, it is like sending a message. Someone sends the message inside an envelope, and someone else receives it and starts doing what the message told him to do."

Sumant watches the example. There is a dog and a pig. The dog barks first and sends a message to the pig. When the pig opens the message, she makes an oink noise. The characters react in time to each other's actions. Sumant thinks this is too complicated. He can just use the wait block, which he has already used many times.

After getting his tablet, Sumant begins a new project. It is ScratchJr free time, and he will make an epic battle from *Pokémon*, his favorite TV show. He decides to use the wait block instead of the newly learned send message block. Until now, every time he created a battle, he had struggled to make his characters react to each other's actions at the right time, but after a lot of trial and error, he always got them to work.

On the internet, he finds pictures of Pokémon for his battle, takes pictures of them, and makes them into ScratchJr characters using the character creation tool. He then choreographs the first

Pokémon's attack, inserting a wait block so that the other Pokémon can avoid it at exactly the right moment. He starts the second Poké-mon's evasion with a green flag, and, eager to watch his progress, he presses the green flag at the top of the screen to see what will happen.

Sumant quickly runs into the same timing problem he always encountered. The avoiding character begins its movements well before the attacking one. Sumant frowns and tries running the program again. When this does not work, he tries everything he can think of to solve the timing problem. He reads his program out loud, counts how many seconds the character should wait before running away from the attack, and makes a new Pokémon charac-ter. Nothing works. He cannot get the timing right.

His teacher, Mr. Jones, happens to walk by his table and notices Sumant's frustration. "Sumant, are you okay?" he asks. Sumant sighs. "I just can't get my project to work, and I wanted to make a really cool Pokémon battle," he responds. "That sounds awesome!" Mr. Jones says, "What can't you figure out?" Sumant shows him his problem, and Mr. Jones nods in understanding. "Sumant, have you thought of using the send message block we learned today? I think that will solve your timing issue," he adds by pointing to the screen and then continues to check on the other children's progress.

Mr. Jones words fill him with a second wind, and Sumant decides to give it a try and experiment with this new approach: the send message block. The problem is that when his teacher was explain-ing how it worked, Sumant was not paying attention. He was not ready then to learn anything new since he assumed that he was going to use the wait block again for his battle. Sumant watches over his friend's project to see if he can understand how she is using the send message block. He notices that there are *two* types of enve-lopes; some blocks have open envelopes and some have closed ones. Suddenly, he remembers what his teacher said: "send mes-sage" always comes with "receive message." They work together.

Sumant decides to try that out and makes a new project with a very simple program. He does not want to mess up his *Pokémon* battle. It works. He is happy and goes back to his *Pokémon* battle to debug it. He watches with delight as the characters move in perfect step with one another. With a surge of reassurance, he begins to code the rest of the battle, pausing to think and test out solutions every time he hits another roadblock. After he finishes the code and designs the background, Sumant smiles widely as the battle comes to life on the screen. The timing is just perfect, he thinks, now knowing why the send message block was a better option than the wait block.

Although reluctant to try anything new at the beginning, Sumant was able to have an open mind and revise the approach he was using for his project until it worked the way he wanted. Motivation played a key role in Sumant's change of attitude; he wanted the project to work exactly as he had planned. Mr. Jones gave him a hint of where to look for the problem but did not solve it for him. He gave him positive feedback and encouraged him to be flexible in his solution. Mr. Jones knows that not all of his students are as willing to consider new ideas as Sumant. Some of them give up, and some of them get frustrated. Some of them demand instant help and gratification. Mr. Jones knows his students well, and he intentionally adjusts how much guidance he gives to each of them based on how open they are to try new things. His own goal is that by the end of the year, if he can tap into every student's personal motivations, all of them will grow the ability to be flexible.

Perseverance
Noun: persistence in a course of action in spite of difficulty or adversity; determination in pursuing goals; firmness of purpose; grit; belief that we can improve

Josué is a second grader who loves to make up stories. Whenever he gets to school early, he rushes to the bin with the dolls and action figures and enacts the stories in his head. He tells his teacher, Ms. Barnard, that when he grows up, he will make really long stories.

Yet, during the ScratchJr CAL curriculum, during which there are many chances for creating stories, he does not. Ms. Barnard is consistently surprised that Josué does not take the opportunity. He seems to enjoy himself, but he uses the time to practice the coding blocks they learned that day instead of creating a story.

One day, as he takes his tablet to his desk, Ms. Barnard approaches him. "Josué," she asks, "You're such a wonderful storyteller. Have you ever considered creating one of your stories with ScratchJr?" Josué's eyes widen. "I'm not sure. In ScratchJr there are only four pages, but my stories have many pages," he responds. "Let me think about this. There might be a way." Ms. Barnard smiles. She has seen projects done with multiple tablets before.

The following day, she walks over to Josué and explains, "I checked the website and I learned that if you use more than one tablet to tell your story, then you could just have your characters go from tablet to tablet when you need more pages. Each tablet can have four pages, so you can just keep adding tablets and you will have a very long story." Josué thinks about this. He loves the idea of using multiple tablets, but that seems like a lot of work. Ms. Barnard smiles again and says, "Of course, I am sure it will be a lot of work, but you could have a really long story like you talked about. Let me know if you need more tablets."

Josué does not like challenges, but he wants to make his story. It is about a prince who loses his kingdom to an evil dragon and must slowly make his way back to defeat the dragon and become king again. Josué gets to work and spends the first fifteen minutes designing the story's main characters and settings. By the end of the lesson, he has only just begun programming the first scene. "How did it go?" Ms. Barnard asks after walking over to him. "It was fun, but I think it could take me a really, really long time to finish it. I'm not even close!" he tells her. "I'll bet that's true," Ms. Barnard muses, "but I also bet it will be amazing when it's finished."

This is the thought that carries Josué forward as he continues working on his project. Every time he uses ScratchJr, it is all he focuses on; whenever the class learns a new block, he finds a way to incorporate it into his story so he can keep working on it with each lesson. In one scene, he wants a wizard to help the prince get into his castle by creating an explosion and bursting open the entrance to a tunnel. When he envisions the spell traveling across tablet screens, shooting to the prince's rescue from a distance, he knows how to make it happen; they learned about recording today, and he can easily record the sound of the spell and make it vanish on one screen and reappear on the next.

After struggling to figure out how to make the wizard look like he cast a spell, Josué decides to make a shooting star character on both screens to represent a beam of magic. When the first one travels to the edge of its screen, he wants the second one to appear and travel across its own screen, ultimately making the explosion. But Josué quickly finds out that the timing for this is impossible. No matter when he presses it, there is always a slight lag in the transition between screens. He keeps trying until Ms. Barnard gives a five-minute warning. Josué slumps back in frustration. "I'm never going to get this right," he frets. Dispirited, he decides to stop working on his story for the day.

The next day, though, their class covers coordination blocks. They can make characters speed up, slow down, stop entirely, or wait to continue their code. Once again, Josué's mind is bursting with ideas. Not only can he now make the spell travel across the screens in the blink of an eye, but he can also make the second shooting star wait until the perfect moment to begin its code by simply pressing the green flags at the same time on both tablets. He spends a long time trying to get the timing right, but when he finally does it, he is left with a seamless transition between the screens and excitedly continues the rest of his story.

"You're so creative, Josué," says Ms. Barnard. "Look at the amazing things you can do when you don't give up!" Each day, she celebrates the smaller accomplishments, which propels him to keep going. The full project takes him two weeks to complete. When he is ready, Ms. Barnard asks him if he wants to project his story onto the white board and show it to the class. He nods energetically. The cheers of his classmates fill the room as they are taken on an adventure with Josué's prince. They jump up and down when they watch the wizard's spell zap across the screens with its sound. Josué leaves school that day bursting with pride. He cannot wait for the next time they use ScratchJr so he can work on a new story.

In the coding playground, it does not matter how long it takes to create a project. Teachers want children to develop persistence. Thus, longer and more difficult projects that are exciting and personally meaningful are a good opportunity.

Alan Kay, a pioneer in the development of the personal computer, coined the phrase "hard fun" to describe an activity that engages us because it is both enjoyable and challenging. In the coding playground, children learn to have hard fun and to manage frustration. Some teachers set up a culture in which succeeding the first time is a rarity. Others remind students that a project will fail a hundred times before it works, thus anticipating the inevitable. This creates a safe learning environment. It happens to everyone; we learn from failure and need to keep trying. Some of the best teachers I have seen over the years invite laughter over failure. Just as children laugh at their mistakes on the playground, they can find silliness in their bugs in the coding playground.

Patience
Noun: the capacity to accept or tolerate delay, trouble, or suffering without getting angry or upset

Today marks the second day that Shreya and Falyn will use the KIBO robot in their kindergarten class. Their teacher, Ms. Shah, noticed yesterday that Falyn was taking a long time to scan, whereas Shreya picked it up fairly quickly. She hoped that by partnering them up, Shreya might help Falyn. Once the girls sit down with their KIBO, they begin programming right away. They are only experimenting with motion blocks, but before they know it, they have put together a short sequence of movements for KIBO to follow.

"Can I scan first?" Shreya asks eagerly. "Okay," Falyn agrees, "but I get to scan next!" Ms. Shah had told them that they should take turns scanning so that everyone is treated fairly and has a chance. Shreya begins scanning each block one by one, quickly moving on as soon as KIBO beeps. "Do you want to press the button?" she offers her friend. Falyn nods excitedly and presses the triangle-shaped start button to launch KIBO into the moving sequence they programmed together.

"Yay!" The girls shout. They begin making another program for Falyn to scan. This one is a little longer; there are about ten wooden blocks for Falyn to get through. She starts by holding KIBO above the begin block, making the red light from the scanner touch the block. Shreya notices that the scanner is touching the center of the block and the red line is not running across the barcode. It does not work. "Try putting it on the black and white lines," Shreya suggests immediately. With difficulty, Falyn moves the red scanning line to the barcodes. It does not work either, but after what feels like an eternity to Shreya, KIBO beeps in affirmation.

Falyn moves to the next block. Shreya notices that the scanner is very diagonal and only cuts through the middle of the barcode rather than running straight through it. Seconds go by, and Falyn moves KIBO's scanner within a centimeter of the block; Shreya knows that this is too close to work. At this point, Shreya notices that their classmates have begun to make more intricate programs. She rests her chin in her hands, remembering how quickly she had scanned through the first program.

"Can I help you?" she asks warily. "No, I want to do it," Falyn says. Shreya groans as Falyn continues to move the scanner up and down without much success. Shreya cannot take it anymore. She snatches the KIBO out of Falyn's hands and begins to scan the program herself. "Hey!" Falyn cries, reaching to get it back. "You're taking ten million years! It'll be faster this way!" Shreya retorts. "But it is my turn!" Falyn shouts back.

Ms. Shah hears the girls shouting and rushes over. "What's going on?" she asks them, looking concerned. "Shreya stole KIBO right out of my hands!" Falyn exclaims. Ms. Shah raises her eyebrows and asks, "Shreya, is this true? Remember, we need to take care of KIBO so it doesn't break." Shreya sighs and replies, "Yes, but she was taking up the whole time trying to scan the blocks!" Ms. Shah asks Shreya to come to the side with her. The two go to a table where the other students cannot hear their conversation and they sit down together. "Shreya, do you play any sports?" asks Ms. Shah. "Yes," Shreya nods, "I like to play tennis." Ms. Shah smiles. "Good! Do you remember the first time you ever played?" Shreya takes a moment to think and then nods. She started taking lessons last summer. Ms. Shah asks, "Was it easy for you to get the ball over the net?" Shreya shakes her head. She remembers how embarrassed she felt that most children were able to return the coach's balls except her. "Sometimes it takes time and practice to get good at something," says Ms. Shah. "Falyn will get better at scanning, just like you did at tennis. She needs time to practice. You need to be patient."

Shreya thinks about this for a moment and then nods in agreement. She remembers how long it took her to hit a ball over the net. Disappointed, she realizes that it will be a long time until Falyn learns to scan. "Okay, Ms. Shah." As Shreya makes her way back over to Falyn, she notices that her friend already stopped holding KIBO too close to the blocks and has made it through a few more of them. "Sorry, Falyn," Shreya says. "It's okay," her friend smiles. "If you try holding it so that the red goes straight through the barcode, it might beep faster," Shreya offers. Falyn tries it, but it still takes her a little while to get KIBO oriented correctly. Shreya does not say anything; she waits and lets her friend figure it out for herself. Eventually, KIBO beeps and Falyn goes through the last few blocks much more quickly. "You did it!" Shreya smiles. The girls high five and begin to watch KIBO perform its sequence.

In the coding playground, patience is an important skill that is developed over time. In this case, patience involved a girl respecting her friend's own learning time. In other cases, it is about patience with one's own self, allowing time to learn. Regardless, patience does not come easily to young children. In an environment in which competition rules, patience will be easily forgotten in the palette of virtues. However, that is not the case in the coding playground in which the outcome is meaningful expression, not speed or efficiency.

Optimism

Noun: hopefulness and confidence about the future or a successful outcome; expecting the best

First grader Jordan is dreading playing with ScratchJr today. Yesterday, the first day his class used the app, he did not pay much attention. He was too hungry, and his mind kept wandering. As a result, today he is totally lost sitting with the iPad in front of him. He has tried stringing blocks together, but for some reason, they will not work. While his classmates begin experimenting, he cannot even start. Fear of being the only person who does not understand keeps creeping back into his mind, and he becomes more disappointed.

Jordan is completely stuck. He is not really sure what the many blocks mean; they simply look like strange symbols to him. Looking around, he notices that his classmates have all already begun making their characters do interesting things. "That looks so cool," he tells his friend April, whose character is growing and shrinking. When he looks at his friend Xavier's iPad, he notices that he has already designed two of his own characters and they are having a conversation. Jordan half-heartedly begins dragging blocks onto the screen, but no matter where he moves them or how he taps, nothing happens. Finally, he pushes his iPad away and puts his head down on his desk, giving up.

"Jordan?" Ms. Shin sees Jordan looking defeated and walks over to him. "Are you done programming?" He looks up to find his teacher's warm eyes looking at him. "I'm not good at ScratchJr," he says frowning. "What do you mean?" she asks. Jordan exclaims, "I can't do it! No matter what I do, it never works." Ms. Shin thinks for a moment and then smiles. "Do you want to know a secret?" she asks. Jordan nods. "No one is supposed to be good at something they've never done before. You've gotten so great at the things you've practiced this year, like reading, or basketball at recess. I'll bet anything that you can do it." Jordan looks skeptical, but he turns back to his iPad. "Do you remember how we learned to start a ScratchJr program?" asks Ms. Shin. Jordan shakes his head. "That's okay!" she says. "We use a green flag block. Do you think you can find that for me?"

Jordan clicks through the many tabs until he finds the green flag block and drags it with difficulty. "Okay, that's our beginning; now the blocks you attach to it will be the middle, and the red end block will be the last." Jordan drags whatever blocks he can find next to the green flag. Ms. Shin directs him to press the green flag in the top corner of the app. When he does, his character begins moving, growing, shrinking, and spinning, just like his classmates' characters. Jordan's face lights up. "See? I knew you could do it. The only thing that stops you is when you think that you can't." Ms. Shin smiles at him. He smiles back. As the class continues using ScratchJr throughout the year, Jordan needs extra help. However, he does not let himself get daunted. He knows that he can learn if he puts his mind and heart into it. His final project is simple but very creative (see figure 7.3)

Some children are naturally optimistic, and others are not. It is the same with teachers. Some trust their students will achieve success if given the right conditions and help, and others have doubts. In the coding playground, the belief that one can learn and grow plays an important role in the learning process. Dweck calls this a

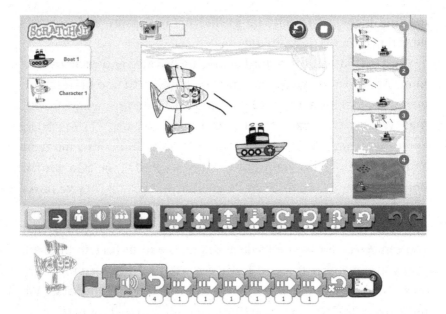

Figure 7.3
Jordan's final ScratchJr project

"growth mindset" as opposed to a "fixed mindset." Individuals who believe that their talents can be developed through hard work, good strategies, and input from others have a growth mindset. They tend to achieve more than those with a more fixed mindset or those who believe their talents are innate gifts. In the coding playground, optimism or a positive attitude toward achieving one's goals makes for a better learning experience. Although teachers are aware this is not an innate characteristic of every student in their class, by understanding optimism as a virtue in the palette, they can intentionally design situations to reinforce and practice it.

Honesty
Noun: the quality of being honorable; rectitude; uprightness; integrity

Today is a big day in Lola's second-grade class; after a semester of working with KIBO, it is finally time for the class to begin their big final projects. For the past few weeks, Lola's class has been reading *Where the Wild Things Are* and discussing the sequence of the story. At the same time, they have explored all of the programming blocks and the KIBO sensors. Lola can use repeats and conditionals, nested loops, and light sensors. She is an expert, and now it is time to put all of that knowledge together. "Today," Mr. Watkins begins, "We're going to plan for our projects in our design journals and then program our own wild rumpuses!" Lola's friend Maria gasps and turns to her excitedly. "I know exactly what I want to do!" she whispers. Lola smiles back but does not say anything. She has no idea what she would do but is hopeful that her creativity will flow once she puts pencil to paper. The wild rumpus is a big party that the story characters throw at the end of the book. Lola and her classmates have been asked to create their own party and write a story about what happens in their design journals, and later they will program the KIBOs to enact it.

Lola loves parties, and she is looking forward to creating her own. But when she sits at her desk to write in her design journal, nothing comes to mind. Every now and again, she writes something down, stares at it, and scribbles it out. As their time for planning winds down, she only has a couple of ideas written on her page, and she does not like them. "Let's plan for five more minutes, and then we can start programming," announces Mr. Watkins. "Remember to share your ideas with your neighbor for feedback!" At this point, chatter breaks out across the room.

Lola realizes with dismay that she has nothing to share. Out of the corner of her eye, she notices that Maria's design journal is filled to the brim with ideas. Lola imagines being the only student without a final project idea. Gulping, she quietly glances over at Maria's journal and tries to make out the words. She writes down everything she sees, deciding that she will just program it differently so no one can tell that the ideas came from her friend. "Okay, everyone!" Mr. Watkins calls over the quiet chatter in the room.

"I'm going to start calling everyone by table to line up and get your KIBOs. You will be programming in pairs! But first, you each need to share your ideas written in the design journal. Discuss them and choose what to do."

When Lola sits on the floor with Maria, blocks sprawled out in front of her, she still does not know what to say. She wrote down ideas like "drinking fruit punch," "eating cake," and "dancing," but she never had a vision for how to translate those ideas into code because they were not hers. She starts worrying that any attempt at incorporating them into her program will not make sense, and she glances at Maria's choice of blocks as guilt swells in her chest. Slowly, she begins copying Maria's program. As the two girls work side by side, Maria cannot help but notice what is going on. "Lola! Why are you copying me?" Maria asks, folding her arms over her chest. "I'm not!" Lola says quickly. Maria glares at her incredulously as her hand shoots into the air. Lola is speechless as Mr. Watkins makes his way over to the two friends and crouches down to talk to them.

"Mr. Watkins," Maria begins, "Lola says she isn't copying my program, but she is! Look, her code is exactly the same as mine, but it's shorter!" Lola's heart starts racing as Mr. Watkins looks back and forth between their codes. "Lola, is this true?" he asks. Lola looks at him but does not say anything, afraid of what will happen if she admits what she did. "You're not in trouble, but it's important to tell the truth so we can make this better," he assures her. Lola pauses and then stares at the floor. "Sorry," she says, "I just couldn't figure out what to write, and I got scared that I wouldn't be able to make anything and then I would have nothing to share." Mr. Watkins smiles encouragingly and tells her, "Thank you for apologizing and for telling the truth."

He turns to Maria and asks, "Maria, do you think you can help your friend? What did you do to come up with your project idea?" Maria's face brightens and answers, "I wrote down everything I could remember from my birthday party last month! Yours was really fun too, Lola." Lola starts remembering the day; she and her friends went swimming, played hide and seek, and even knocked over a piñata! "Does that help you think of some ideas for the wild rumpus party, Lola?" Mr. Watkins asks. She nods, a big smile forming on her face. Lola takes the rest of the day to replan her project. Next time, whenever she cannot decide what to write, she shares with her friend that she has hit a roadblock and asks for help brainstorming.

When confronted by Maria and her teacher, Lola chose to take the high road, confess, and apologize. She was able to come forward because Mr. Watkins set up a classroom environment in which honesty was deeply valued. In the coding playground, the teacher's values have as much of an impact as the children's values. Those need to be made explicit so children know what to expect. When I work with teachers on CAL professional development, I make sure teachers spend time exploring their own palette of virtues and how those relate to the values in the coding playground. That is the only possible way for them to later bring the palette of virtues into their classrooms.

Fairness
Noun: impartial and just treatment without favoritism or discrimination; justice

"Okay everyone, find your KIBO partners and line up to get your robots and blocks!" Ms. Alvarez announces to her kindergarten class. "Today, we'll get to have KIBO free play!" Excited whispers ripple through the room; the students had only used KIBO a few times up until now and only ever to do projects the teacher gave them, like programming KIBO to dance the Hokey Pokey or follow a maze. Everyone has been waiting for the chance to play with their own ideas. "Remember," Ms. Alvarez says, "there are four of you working with each KIBO. Everyone is in charge of making sure all partners get a turn programming, a turn building, a turn scanning, and a turn decorating the robot." Kentaro, Taylor, Briana, and Carl are group one. They negotiate who will take which role first. "Kentaro, I have an idea!" Taylor exclaims as they get their robot. "Do you want to pretend KIBO is a car for some of the toys?" she asks. Kentaro's face brightens. "Yeah, that would be so cool!" Briana agrees, but Carl does not seem that interested in the choice of project.

On their way over to the bin of toys, Kentaro and Taylor talk excitedly about their ideas. As they place their things down and find the toys they want as passengers, they notice that Briana has already started putting together a sequence of blocks. "Maybe we should test what we have so far," suggests Kentaro. "Good idea!" says Taylor. She reaches for KIBO and begins scanning each barcode. "Can I press the start button?" Carl asks. But as soon as he finishes his sentence, Taylor has already pressed KIBO's blinking green triangle and launched it into its program. "Hey! I wanted to do that!" Carl protests. "Sorry!" Taylor says. "I was closest to KIBO, so I got to press it." Kentaro stays silent and privately vows to be closest to KIBO next time.

The four children start to negotiate whose turn it is to be the programmer next. After a few more minutes of work, Taylor picks up KIBO. "I think we should test again!" she says, beginning to scan each block. "Taylor! I was closest to KIBO, so that means I get to scan it this time!" Kentaro shouts. Taylor shrugs. "Well, I'm already holding it, so it's just easier," she explains, beginning to scan each block. When she puts KIBO on the ground, Kentaro jumps toward it to try to press the green start button, but Taylor gets there first. "No fair!" he shouts. "You never let me scan the blocks or press start!" He reaches for KIBO again, but Carl snatches it before he gets there. "Stop, Carl!" Taylor turns her body to prevent him from getting KIBO. "Fine," he says, standing up. He then walks to the corner of the room and sits down, burying his face in his knees and hugging them to his chest.

Taylor keeps working with the other children for a few minutes. Before she knows it, though, Carl is walking toward them. This time, Ms. Alvarez is with him. "Taylor," their teacher begins, "Carl told me what happened. Can you tell me your side of the story?" Taylor nods and explains that Carl got upset and ran away because he did not get a chance to scan the programs or press the start button. "But it was just always closer to me, so I always scanned with it," he explains. "Hmm," Ms. Alvarez says, "Taylor, how would you feel if you never got to scan with KIBO, even though you wanted to?" Taylor thinks about this for a moment and then looks down. "Sad," she admits.

"Do you remember when I said to make sure everyone got a turn? Why do you think that's an important rule?" asks Ms. Alvarez. Briana, who was distracted drawing little passengers to put in the toy cars, lifts her head and responds, "So that no one gets sad that they don't get a turn." Ms. Alvarez nods and then addresses all four children. "Right. What can we do to make sure that everyone is happy when playing together?" she asks. Kentaro thinks for a moment. "We can take turns," Taylor proposes. "Does this sound like a good plan to all of you?" asks Ms. Alvarez. They all nod.

Next Ms. Alvarez helps them write down a turn-taking schedule so they would not forget who has each job and when they switch jobs. As a five-year-old, it is not easy to remember four different roles and who comes after whom. Despite the large number of children in a group having to share one KIBO, due to the lack of classroom resources, this is an opportunity to explore civility. This sequencing exercise is not only about fairness but also aligns with the core computer science concept taught in kindergarten: an algorithm is a list of instructions that a robot or program will follow. In this case, creating a list of orderly jobs becomes another way to explore the precursor of algorithms: order matters in a sequence. This applies for both computers and for people.

Generosity

Noun: the quality of being kind; giving and receiving, helping self and others

Mikah is six years old, and she looks forward to playing with KIBO at school. Today, her kindergarten class is learning about the repeat block: a block that makes KIBO perform the same series of actions multiple times. Before the class breaks into partners to practice what they have learned, Mikah's teacher announces that everyone is going to use the repeat block to program a dance for KIBO. She adds, "At the end of the hour, all KIBOs will come together to attend a dance party at the front of the room." At this news, Mikah and her partner Javier look at each other excitedly. They quickly begin brainstorming their KIBO's dance and work together to start building the program. It takes them a few tries to get it right, and before they know it, Mikah and Javier put the blocks in the right order. KIBO spins and twirls over and over again. They add colorful lights and are about to experiment with the sound sensor.

As they are working on their project, Mikah is approached by Ms. Tanaka, who kneels beside her. "Mikah," she whispers, "I noticed that Alexander looks very upset. Would you mind seeing what's wrong for me?" Mikah searches the room for Alexander and realizes immediately that Ms. Tanaka is right. Alexander is crying, his arms are crossed, and he is facing away from his KIBO. Mikah nods and then turns to Javier. "I'll be right back," she says. "Okay!" he responds. Mikah walks over to her friend and asks him what is wrong. "I can't do it!" Alexander mumbles. "I've tried scanning my program so many times, but it won't work." Alexander's partner is absent today, so he is working by himself. "Hmm," Mikah muses. She does not like seeing her friend look so sad. "Can you show me? Maybe I can help." Alexander takes his KIBO and scans the program. As he scans each barcode, Mikah covers the surrounding blocks with her hands to make sure he scans them in the right order. Everything seems to be going fine, but when KIBO scans the end block, it makes a noise their teacher warned them about. It means that KIBO cannot understand the code. "See?" Alexander looks at Mikah dejectedly. "I can't figure it out."

Mikah thinks for a moment. Suddenly, a lightbulb goes off in her head; she realizes that Alexander is making the same mistake that she and Javier had made earlier. "Wait a minute!" she exclaims. "I know what's wrong! You forgot to put the end repeat block at the end of what you want KIBO to repeat. That way KIBO knows when to stop repeating." Alexander's eyes grow wide, remembering this from the lesson. "Oh!" he realizes. Mikah goes over to the bin, digs for the end repeat block, and hands it to Alexander. After putting it where he wants it in the program, Alexander rescans the code as Mikah covers the surrounding barcodes again. This time, KIBO does not make the error sound, and its triangle flashes green. Alexander presses the triangle, and KIBO launches into his dance routine, repeating it four times.

Earlier on, as Ms. Tanaka walked the room to see students' progress, she noticed that Alexander was frustrated. By looking over his shoulder, she quickly understood the bug in his code. It was a simple syntax issue. At that point, Ms. Tanaka had a choice to make on her own: quickly help Alexander by handing him the missing end repeat block or find another child in the class who was already an expert with repeat blocks and could figure this out. The latter was more time-consuming for Ms. Tanaka and was also riskier. Ms. Tanaka suspected that Mikah was going to be able to help Alexander. She knew Mikah had the needed skills, both technically and emotionally. However, maybe Mikah could not help Alexander in time to prevent a meltdown, or maybe Mikah would refuse to leave her own project and spend time with someone else's. Despite these maybes, from the point of view of promoting generosity, calling a child to help another is a win-win situation. Even if things did not work out as expected, there was still an opportunity to address so many other aspects of socioemotional development. Ms. Tanaka knew all of this when she called on Mikah, who had mastered repeat blocks, to go help Alexander.

Later that day, when Ms. Tanaka asked the class to stop their robotics work and get out their collaboration webs, Mikah was proud to draw a line from her name to Alexander's name. She had helped a friend that day. Alexander did the same in his own collaboration web, but the arrow had a different direction. He had received help. In the coding playground, setting up situations for children to help each other is seen as an act of generosity and not only teamwork. There is intentionality in asking children to help someone outside of their team.

Gratitude

Noun: the quality of being thankful; readiness to show appreciation; being aware of good things

Today is a special day in Gabriela's second-grade class. Ms. Daniels announces at the beginning of coding class that they will get to play freeze dance, which is Gabriela's favorite game. During the first round, Gabriela has lots of fun jumping around with her classmates, expecting the music to stop at any second. After they end, Ms. Daniels says that everyone will program their own freeze dance on ScratchJr by using the "wait" block, a command that causes a character to stop in the middle of its program for a certain amount of time.

Gabriela vows to make her best program yet in honor of her favorite game. Gabriela usually likes to share what she creates during technology circle, and today she wants to share more than ever. "As you program, think about the things you like about your project," Ms. Daniels instructs. "Everyone is going to talk about the part of their project that they're most happy about."

Once she gets her tablet, Gabriela gets right to work. First, she draws a character that looks like a speaker and uses the sound recorder block to record herself singing. Occasionally, she cuts her-self off mid-word and stops singing to represent the "freezes" in the music. Then, she creates an intricate party room as her setting. She takes her time adding small details and creating a sparkling disco ball, a glowing dance floor, and even a turntable for a DJ. Her older brother has one and explained to her how it works. Then, she begins drawing the rest of her characters. She wants at least three characters that do their own separate dances and a DJ running the show in the background. That will be her older brother. Tomorrow, she will take a picture of him and bring it to school to incorpo-rate into the project. For now, she takes her time drawing the other characters, giving each of them a different costume to wear at her dance club. Exactly as she is finishing her third character, she hears Ms. Daniels call out, "We're going to start sharing in about five minutes!"

Gabriela's heart starts racing. She had become so engrossed in her project that she completely lost track of time! Quickly, she decides that she will not design a DJ and begins to code all the characters' separate dances. She knows it will take her much longer than five minutes to make up a good dance move for each of her characters. She works as quickly as she can and thoughtfully drags blocks onto the screen. As she thinks she is almost done, she frantically remem-bers that she needs to time the wait blocks to freeze the characters at the same time as the music. "Okay everyone, it's time to start wrapping up!" her teacher calls.

Gabriela only has one character's dance programmed, and it only has one wait block that is not even synced with the music. The other two characters are totally static and have no programs. As her classmates start sharing their dances, Gabriela tries to keep working in secret. "Gabriela, it's time to listen to our friends," her teacher calls. Gabriela takes one last look at her incomplete project before slumping onto the floor, dismayed. She will not be able to share her project during technology circle. When the class is done reflecting and begins putting the tablets away, Ms. Daniels looks up to find Gabriela crouched by her desk. "What's wrong, Gabriela? You're usually one who likes to share her project," she asks, smiling. Gabriela explains that she could not get to finish her project on time. "Can I see what you have so far?" Ms. Daniels asks.

Gabriela shows her the tablet. "Wow, I see lots of fantastic detail in this project! What's your favorite part about it?" asks Ms. Daniels, since Gabriela did not get to share with the class. "It would have been the freeze dance and my brother, the DJ," Gabriela mutters, sadly. Ms. Daniels pauses for a moment. "Hmm, well what's the favorite part that you did make?" Gabriela looks again at her project, reconsidering it. "Well, I like the setting I drew for the background a lot. I like the spot for the DJ and the disco ball, but I don't have my brother's picture here," she admits. "And you had great ideas for the project, right? Even though you didn't have time to do them?" Ms. Daniels asks. Gabriela nods in response. "Isn't it amazing that you came up with those ideas?" Gabriela smiles widely at her teacher. "If you want, next time there is free time in class, you can continue working on this project. I will save it for you. Bring your brother's picture tomorrow." Ms. Daniels knows that even though Gabriela did not get to finish her dance on time, she had put a lot of effort and cared deeply about it. There was a lot to acknowledge about what she accomplished. "Thank you, Ms. Daniels," she says. She puts her tablet away feeling proud of what she created and grateful for getting an opportunity to share it as soon as she is finished with it.

The CAL pedagogy trains teachers to become aware of the good things that happen in the coding playground and recognize them. Sometimes that means making exceptions, deviating from a well-designed plan, or delaying final outcomes. Coding is hard. It requires time and commitment, dealing with frustration, and engaging in difficult problem solving. In addition, when creating projects that are personally meaningful, one might get so absorbed in some of the details that time flies by quickly.

The well-known psychologist Mihaly Csikszentmihalyi proposed the concept of flow, a highly focused mental state conducive to productivity, to describe experiences such as the one Gabriela had. The intense and focused concentration on the present moment, the sense of personal control and agency over her project, and the loss of time and experiencing the activity as intrinsically rewarding are all aspects of being in a state flow, where nothing else matters. Gabriela was engrossed in drawing and programming her dance party, and Ms. Daniels recognized this and was grateful for it. What more can a second-grade teacher wish for than one of her students putting all of her heart, brain, and soul into making a project?

The CAL pedagogy, which engages children in learning to use the language of coding to express themselves in personally meaningful ways, seeks to nurture flow experiences. It recognizes and appreciates them by welcoming flexibility around the day's schedule. Unfortunately, class times are generally broken into forty-five-minute slots and creativity cannot be corralled nor rushed. Just like in the physical playground, where children often want to stay longer, in the coding playground we hope for children to get so absorbed and engaged in their projects that they lose track of time. As they grow, they will learn about time management and meeting deadlines. In this vignette, Ms. Daniels recognized that Gabriela was not procrastinating but was fully engaged in her project. The coding playground strives for a balance between the challenge of the task and the skill of the performer. If the task is too easy or too difficult, flow cannot occur. However, when achieved, both teachers and students are grateful.

Gratitude is not only about children thanking those teachers or peers who provide technical help but also about recognizing when they alter their plans to accommodate a particular need or passion. Gratitude is one of the most important elements in forging long-lasting I–Thou relationships.

Forgiveness

Noun: the action of pardoning and accepting, giving a second chance to self and others

Yakov and Annie have been best friends since kindergarten, and today they get to be KIBO partners. They just listened to their teacher read the book *There Was an Old Lady Who Swallowed a Fly*, a story about an old woman who swallows a fly and continues to swallow increasingly large animals as the story progresses. After finishing the book, Yakov and Annie's teacher, Mr. Arambulo, announces that today's KIBO project is to program the robot to act like the old lady from the story. Pictures of each animal she swallows line the floor, and the students have to make KIBO visit each animal and perform an action to indicate that it is "swallowing" the animal it reaches.

As Yakov and Annie begin coding together, they figure out how to get KIBO to approach the fly. It takes three forward blocks. Annie scans the blocks and places KIBO on the floor. Yakov then presses the start button. After KIBO makes its way to the fly, it is time to decide what it will do to convey that it swallows it. "I think KIBO should sing because we sing along when we read the book!" Annie exclaims, referring to the tune used to turn the book's words into a song. "No way," Yakov shakes his head. "She needs to swallow the fly, not sing to the fly. It should get to the fly and shake so it looks like it's eating it!" Annie furrows her brow and crosses her arms. "No! I want it to sing," she insists. "No! Shaking is way better," Yakov says. Annie snaps, "If we don't do the singing, then I don't want to do KIBO with you anymore!" Silence fills the space between the pair for a moment. "Fine," Yakov says, and he begins to collect all the sing blocks and put them behind him so she can't reach them. "Yakov!" she cries. "Give them back!" Yakov does not do anything and continues to protest. "Ugh!" she shouts, finally giving up on getting the blocks back from him. The two face away from each other angrily.

"Yakov? Annie? Are you done making your program?" The partners look up to find Mr. Arambulo. "Annie says she doesn't want to do KIBO with me anymore," Yakov says bitterly. "That's because Yakov took all of the sing blocks, and he won't let me use them!" retorts Annie. Mr. Arambulo crouches down to talk to them and asks them to tell him the full story, one at a time. Once he is finished hearing both sides, he thinks for a moment. "Annie, would you like it if Yakov said he didn't want to play with you anymore?" he asks. Annie stares at the floor and shakes her head. "Yakov, would you like it if someone took all the blocks you wanted to use?" asks Mr. Arambulo. "No," Yakov admits. "Friends upset each other all the time," Mr. Arambulo says, looking at the two. "But now we have to decide what to do next. We can keep being angry, or we can apologize and try to find a way to program KIBO so everyone will be happy. What do you both want to do?"

Yakov and Annie look at each other. Suddenly, Annie is struck with an idea. "Yakov, what if KIBO sings and shakes when it reaches each animal?" A smile runs across Yakov's face. "I really like that!" he says. Mr. Arambulo smiles too and says, "Great job, you two. But I think that Yakov still owes an apology to Annie for taking all of the blocks. Annie, you still owe an apology to Yakov for not wanting to play with him." The pair looks at each other and apologizes. Next, they sit together to keep working on their KIBO project until time runs out. By the end, the old lady KIBO sings and shakes before it eats the fly and the rest of the animals.

In this vignette, forgiveness involves two children who did something wrong and chose to make amends. However, pardoning sometimes involves the self. In the coding playground we have seen many cases in which children are so upset with themselves because they did not catch a syntax error or a simple bug that they cannot move on and continue working. The CAL pedagogy identifies the ability to forgive, oneself, or others as an important value in the palette of virtues.

Coding a Mensch

The ten vignettes just presented reflect multiple experiences in many classrooms over many years of working with both ScratchJr and KIBO. For narrative purposes, I chose to focus each one of them on a particular value in the palette of virtues. I also chose to highlight the teacher's role.

A skeptical reader might wonder what is unique about these classrooms. What is so special about the coding playground and the palette of virtues? In which ways were these teachers handling things differently than in the math or literacy class time? Isn't socioemotional learning one of the most important aspects of schooling? Why do we need coding to remind us of the importance of working with values and promoting character strengths?

Some educators understand that despite the academic subject they are teaching, their goal is to nurture children's socioemotional and ethical lives. These teachers will intentionally promote character development and will take advantage of any opportunity that arises. However, for others, that is not the case. In particular, with the growing movement to delegate computational subjects to specialized technology coaches who only meet with students a few hours a week, we might start to see a divide between the teaching of technical skills and the human dimension. I worry about this. Every time we teach, we have an opportunity and a responsibility to bring about a mensch into the world. The problem solving that naturally occurs in the coding playground is a fertile ground for this.

When programming is viewed as not only an instrumental tool to problem-solve technical challenges but also a symbolic system of representation for creative expression, we enter the realm of human relationships and the possibility of nurturing I–Thou encounters.

A Window into Their World: The Learning Family

It is 1998 in Buenos Aires, Argentina. We were exploring how the LEGO Mindstorms robotic kit, which had been recently commercially released after years of research at the MIT Media Lab, could be used by families to explore values at the Arlene Fern Community School. At the time, the field of educational robotics was emerging.

At the school, a group of parents and children gathered for a week around the time of the Jewish High Holidays, a period of ten days between the Jewish New Year and the Day of Atonement. This timing was carefully chosen due to the spiritual work of reflection and forgiveness that takes place both in the school and the community around the most sacred holidays for Judaism.

The rabbi, Sergio Bergman, was co-leading the robotics workshop with me and Claudia Urrea. On one of the tables, we had placed cards with different values. Some were universal and others were directly related to the Jewish holidays. Each family was invited to choose a value card as inspiration for their robotic project. After the initial training, during which parents and children learned how to use motors and sensors, how to program with the LEGO Mindstorms software, and how to build a sturdy LEGO project, they began working on their choice of project.

At the end of the workshop, right before the Friday's kabbalat shabbat religious service, the projects were displayed in the hallway of the synagogue so congregants can play with them during an open house. In addition, each family prepared a poster telling the story of their work together and wrote a technological prayer, reflecting on their experience and showing gratitude for a specific aspect of their learning. Those technological prayers were photocopied and included in the prayer book to be used that Friday night. Finally, the group wrote a collective prayer together to show gratitude for all the new things they learned and experimented with during the workshop.

Around twenty-five people participated in the workshop. Children were granted special permission from the school principal to miss classes during that week, and parents took time off from work. When evaluating the experience, I grouped the resulting projects into three different categories according to the unique ways in which families used robotics to explore values.

The first category were projects to represent symbols. For example, Michael, a ten-year-old boy, explained, "We built a *Magen David*, Star of David, as a symbol of our Jewish people, and we programmed it to turn forever like the wheel of life and have flashing lights resembling candles welcoming the New Year. We also reproduced the sound of the shofar, an ancient musical instrument typically made of a ram's horn, used for Jewish religious purposes. It has three different tones that are supposed to awake us for reflection and atonement." Michael and his father had chosen the value "awakening" or "call for reflection."

Projects in the second category used robotics to represent abstract values as opposed to concrete symbols. For example, Marcia and her father chose the value of *Teshuvah*, repentance or repairing mistakes. They created a puppet theater in which two friends hug after a fight. Later, I will share more about this project.

The third category involved projects that used robotics to evoke reflection and conversation. For example, Paula and her ten-year-old son Matias created a conveyor belt contraption to transport the actions of the previous year. Paula explained that "during the High Holidays we think about our actions, about what we did right and what we did wrong. It is the time of the year to reflect and become conscious about our past deeds so we can choose to continue in a good direction or to rectify our actions." The conveyor belt was designed to carry actions, represented by foam rubber cubes wrapped in colored paper and labeled, until a reflection point signaled by two sensors. At that time, the conveyor belt would stop so users could spend the needed time to decide whether the action was positive and press the "good" sensor or negative and press the "bad" sensor. After the sensor was pressed, the conveyor belt resumed its movement. An action considered good was transferred to a good container, and an action considered bad was taken back, meaning that people had to amend it.

During the open house for the community, Matias presented the conveyor belt. When playing with the contraption, one of the adult visitors pressed the "good action" touch sensor and observed the action block move forward very slowly. He commented, "I see that the good actions take more time. Since they are good, they should last longer." This reflection about values was triggered by the performance of the mechanics behind the belt structure and engaged everyone in an interesting discussion.

Each of these three different ways of using robotics represents a unique pathway to work with values. Projects in the first category, technology to represent symbols, treated values in a shallow way. People created artifacts that resembled the Jewish symbols without deeper exploration of the nature of the values represented by these symbols. Projects in the second category, technology to represent values, involved both artifacts and stories that made the chosen value more explicit. Projects in the third category used technology to evoke reflection and conversation, treated values in a more elaborated way, and provided an opportunity for others to engage in experiencing the complexity of the chosen values and participate in thoughtful discussion.

Next, I will tell two stories to better understand the difference between the last two categories, which are the most interesting ones, in terms of learning about values. Juan is an engineer who participated with his young daughter. "Pattie and I talked a lot about giving, and we realize that giving is, at the same time, receiving. Through our project we wanted to show that when we give something, we do not exactly know what we are receiving, but we always receive something back," explained Juan. This is a sophisticated concept to understand with words; however, Juan and Pattie started playing with the robotics and arts and crafts materials before they developed a fully functional project idea. Pattie found fabric she liked and wanted to make a moving doll. From this simple idea, father and daughter started to explore how the concept of giving and receiving could be incorporated into a LEGO doll.

After four days of working together, the doll was ready. Pattie explained, "We made a doll with two yellow hands, and every time you give her a present in one hand, she turns around and gives you something back with her other hand. But you don't know what she is giving you. I made little boxes. Inside they have pictures of smiles, flowers, and hugs. So you can't see them. There is a sensor in the empty hand, and when it sees that you gave it something, it makes the motor move, and the doll gives you her other hand with one of the boxes."

The first component of the "giving and receiving" project was the head of the doll, built out of materials they glued and colored (figure 7.4). Pattie took the design lead here but commanded her dad to use the glue gun in ways she was afraid to. The body consisted of gears, which provided strong motion to the rest of the doll, and a motor attached to a rotation sensor that kept track of the turns. Both hands had light sensors and light sources. They used the source to make the light more constant so that the small changes in the light reading were easy to detect. Juan was the lead engineer, and it is not clear if Pattie was able to fully understand what he was doing. It evolved into a complex technical project.

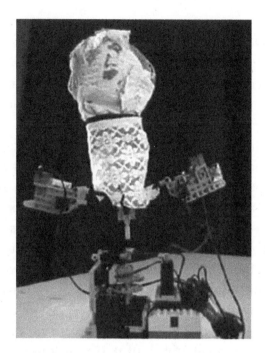

Figure 7.4
A giving and receiving LEGO doll

Juan wrote a program to detect a new object in the receiving hand, make the doll turn to offer a gift with the giving hand, and wait to turn back after it detected the gift was taken. The project's complexity did not overwhelm this pair. They had chosen the value giving and receiving and wanted to have their project display it properly. Pattie did not lose interest, as the idea was mainly hers and the doll was looking good and even becoming alive every time it moved. While father and daughter worked on their project, they were also engaged in a conversation about the nature of giving and receiving and how it relates to the Jewish holidays. Pattie contributed her ideas and Juan his technical skills. They both learned to ask questions and solve problems in a way that the other could understand. They had to learn each other's languages.

In another corner of the room, Marcia and her dad also chose the value of *Teshuvah* but gave it a different interpretation. "This project tells the story of two girls that after a fight give each other a hug and become best friends," explained Marcia. "It is about the *Teshuvah* that allows us to repair our mistakes. The friends did *Teshuvah* and became friends again with a big hug."

To represent this abstract value, the father and daughter created a puppet theater inside a box and installed a curtain that opened to show the performance of two LEGO dolls hugging after a fight. Marcia wrote a play about the girls' situation and narrated in the background as the show started. She built the dolls with LEGO bricks, attached colorful strings as hair, and placed motors in the arms to swing back and forth simulating a hug. Meanwhile her dad, the rabbi of the school, was busy in and out of the classroom. Marcia worked mostly on her own. The project was not as technically sophisticated as Juan and Pattie's but stood out for the abundance of art materials and colorful cloth that Marcia used to create the puppet theater and to dress the dolls.

Marcia had a hard time building and programming the movement of the arms as well as writing the code to control the hug. Her dolls looked as if they were hitting each other instead of hugging. During the first technology circle, when families showed their projects to each other in preparation for the final community open house, Peter, a child participating in the workshop with his mother, told Marcia, "This is not about *Teshuvah*! The dolls are not hugging but slapping each other. They are not sorry. They keep fighting." The young boy was referring to the fact that both arms would not move up at the same speed and would not reach the same altitude. Marcia tried to convince him that he was wrong and, on the spot, came up with a complex explanation of a new type of hug that looks like a slap. But the young boy would not give up. After engaging in a long discussion about what *Teshuvah* is, everyone jumped in and agreed that this project did not represent it. The LEGO dolls did not behave like friends. Marcia was not happy.

The next day she talked with her dad and they agreed that there were two possible solutions. They must either change the story and the value conveyed by the project or work harder on the programming and the mechanics. Her dad agreed to help her and stay in the room with her. However, halfway through the morning, her dad had to leave the classroom again.

Even though Marcia said that she hated programming, she chose to work hard at it because *Teshuvah* was an important value to her. She was not ready to give it up. She debugged her program, asked for help, and played with the mechanics of her contraption until she came up with a movement that looked very much like a hug. She was thrilled!

Marcia's theater, and the fact that it was not working as expected, generated an in-depth discussion about the chosen value. In a different class situation, this philosophical discussion would have been initiated by the teacher (e.g., the teacher telling a story about *Teshuvah* and asking kids to comment on it) or at a very high personal cost (e.g., if there was a fight and the conflict needed to be resolved). In this experience, the personal attachment that Marcia had to the value of *Teshuvah* motivated her to work hard to debug her program and to acquire new technical skills, even if her dad could not help her.

At the end of the week, all of the projects were presented in the open house for the whole community. It was held in the synagogue hall an hour before the religious service started. Community members were invited to walk around, ask questions, play with the projects, and talk with the presenters. Even though the number of visitors kept growing, the open house ended with Rabbi Bergman inviting everyone to sit down to start the traditional religious service.

During the sermon, he referred to the learning experience that occurred during the workshop and connected the act of creation that happened that week with our role as partners in the creation of the world. From the pulpit, he read the collective prayer created by all parents and children: "We, the participants of the Lego–LOGO workshop give thanks because we had the possibility to experiment, to work, and to share new materials with classmates, our parents, and people whom we didn't know before. We were creative and we could build projects that express what we believe, feel, and live by. We played with materials that opened up many new possibilities. We shared within community, and we were able to create while playing."

This experience truly integrated technology and values. Most specifically, it integrated the palette of virtues of the Jewish High Holidays. The robotic projects were used not only to explore and display them but also to evoke conversations about them. Furthermore, the project was truly integrated into the fabric of the school and the synagogue, through an open house for all community members right before the religious service and through the mention in Rabbi Bergman's sermon.

8

Coding Bridges

Jim (seven years old): My fish swims across the screen and a mean shark will eat it.

Gabe (six years old): There is no mean shark in ScratchJr.

Jim: I will make one.

Gabe: Can you make it not very scary?

I am proud of ScratchJr and KIBO. From my time at the MIT Media Lab, I am proud of SAGE and Zora. However, my deep passion, what I think about when I daydream and when I swim in the lake, is not technology. It is children. It is their potential to be happy, to be good people, to connect with others and the world, and to develop a sense of transcendence through I–Thou relationships.

When I finished my doctoral work in 2001, the natural option would have been for me to teach in a computer science or media studies department. However, I chose a child development department. My peers and mentors had a hard time understanding my choice. My response was always the same: I want to make a lasting impact on children and their lives, their families, their communities, and their institutions. Technology is just a tool for me. I want to use it in the service of something else: children.

Now, twenty years later, I do not regret my choice. I have been able to bring my expertise in designing and studying learning technologies to a different discipline. At my DevTech lab in the Eliot-Pearson Department of Child Study and Human Development at Tufts University, I train students to make an impact on the lives of children through technology. They become professors and educational designers; they work in start-ups and ed-tech companies, museums and schools, hospitals, and nonprofits. They understand and use the language of computer science, the maker movement, and educational robotics to design better experiences. They can apply interdisciplinary approaches and research methodologies, and they see the challenges of developmentally appropriate tools and pedagogies and want to make a difference in the world. They also know that, although powerful, the teaching of coding will not be enough to fix the digital gap between those who have access to power, resources, networks, and new devices and those who lack the same access unless structural and complex changes are made to our educational system.

My doctoral mentor at the MIT Media Lab, Seymour Papert, started as a pioneer in the field of artificial intelligence. However, his passion was making machines to help children think better, in contrast to machines that think on their own. That is why he spent time in Geneva, Switzerland, working with Jean Piaget. Papert was adamant about changing the world through his work. He wanted to go beyond observing and describing. He wanted to intervene, to design new learning experiences. And that is what I learned from him.

In this book I presented an approach that brings together the human and the technological, the uniqueness of the written language with what is special about programming languages. While my expertise is in designing technologies, I am deeply interested in integrating those technologies into the design of encounters that build I–Thou relationships. Learning to code is a gateway to learning about each other and about our own selves, and it is an opportunity to build bridges.

In her book *Bring the World to the Child: Technologies of Global Citizenship in American Education*, Katie Day Good documents the history, dating back to the first half of the twentieth century, of using new technologies and emerging media to promote world-minded citizenry and cultural pluralism in education. Magazines, lantern slide projectors, photographs, pen pal correspondence, messenger dolls, scrapbooks, drama pageants, student assemblies, radio, motion pictures, TV, and, most recently, the internet, have all penetrated the imagination of progressive educators. The multisensory and experiential learning of these new media open up opportunities to prepare children for democratic values and global citizenship in a multicultural, multiethnic, and multireligious world.

Over the years, following this long-lasting tradition, I have also developed and run a series of programs that make use of CAL to build local and global bridges. In previous chapters I described my work with the Zora virtual world and SAGE. Here, I am sharing the experiences I have had with robotics, culture, and values with children, families, and educators. Over a span of over twenty years, I used different kinds of robotic kits in many different educational settings. I learned from each one of them and refined the pedagogy as well as the methodologies for evaluating success.

The first program, named Con-science, was in 1998, while I was a graduate student at the MIT Media Lab. I took several LEGO Mindstorms robotic kits to a Jewish school in Argentina and worked with parents and children around the Jewish High Holidays. The vignette in the previous chapter's section "A Window into Their World" tells the story of that project.

Later, when I was starting as a professor at Tufts, I wondered how I could extend that experience and engage families from different religious backgrounds and traditions in a joint exploration. As a result, Project Inter-Actions was born in the early 2000s. Over several weekends, we conducted robotics workshops with a diverse group of over twenty families. Project Inter-Actions workshops helped participants learn robotics by hands-on exploration and by having ample time to learn about each other's cultures and religions. The final challenge was for parents and children to create a robotic project reflecting the family's cultural or religious background to teach others. Some examples are the water scooper from a village in India, a shaking Easter Bunny, a Christmas tree with flashing lights, a hopping Eskimo that recognized different shades of white, and Go-Lem, the matzoh-seeking robot.

Most recently, in 2019, I developed the "Beyond STEM" program that works with KIBO and the CAL pedagogy. Many of the vignettes in this book were taken from this experience in eight secular and religious schools from the three major monotheists religions, Judaism, Christianism, and Islam, in Boston, Massachusetts, and Buenos Aires, Argentina. The project first involved the training of thirty-six kindergarten teachers and school administrators in both cities. Then, they adapted the CAL curriculum to work in their own classrooms over the course of a twelve-week period with a total of 224 children. Over those twelve weeks, through ethnographic observation, focus groups, and surveys, we came to better understand how robotics can be used as a tool for character development in diverse settings and how KIBO and CAL can be tailored to reflect each school's specific palette of virtues.

For example, Our Lady's Academy, a Catholic school in Boston, created a virtues parade as a culminating project. Children programmed their KIBOs to parade through the school hallway displaying colorful balloons. Each balloon had taped on it a virtues card representing one of the nine school values: faith, love, kindness, generosity, courage, honesty, respect, responsibility, and humility (figure 8.1). Balloons whirled around as the KIBOs spun in an infinite loop, and children cackled and jumped up and down as the parade went down the hallway; watching some robots crash into the walls was just part of the process.

Figure 8.1
The virtues parade

At the end of the Beyond STEM project, every school posted their resulting robotic projects on a website to share among all participating schools in both English and Spanish. The teachers were encouraged to peruse the projects made by other schools, show them to their students in their own classrooms, and leave comments for one another. While all of the robotics projects differed in content, technical skills, and art decorations amid religious and cultural differences, educators chose to create robotic projects to express their different identities and talk about their associated challenges. The vignette in this chapter will tell that story.

The Hidden Curriculum

The vision of a world populated by people happy with themselves, deeply tolerant, and respectful to each other is shared by almost everyone. However, in democratic societies, the pairing of values and education is sometimes controversial: Whose values are to be taught? How can we teach and learn multiple and sometimes opposing values? How do we avoid indoctrination without falling in a relativistic perspective? Is it possible to learn about values without exploring identity issues? How does diversity play out in the search for universality?

These questions do not have easy answers. Some educators chose to avoid them by rejecting moral education in schools. Instead, they support civic education and antibias approaches but want to avoid associations with conservative proponents of a moral truth. Others choose to welcome socioemotional learning in their classrooms but shy away from using the term *character development*.

Willingly or unwillingly, however, teachers teach values, and these values are part of the hidden curriculum. The coding playground makes values visible by offering an initial palette of virtues to work with. Most of these values and characteristics are usually displayed by successful programmers and cultures of innovation. Different traditions, societies, and groups might want to add or remove some of them. Others might want to mix and match and prioritize some values and character strengths over others. The intentional teacher makes her own palette with universal and particular elements. In the coding playground, by understanding coding as another language, that is, by situating the activity of programming as a vehicle for expression and communication, children can experience values and develop virtues in the context of forming I–Thou relationships.

STEM educators have identified the potential of computer science to contribute to their disciplines. However, those interested in issues of values and identity are yet to discover how. While games and apps have been designed for this purpose, in this book I show a different pathway: how to intentionally integrate the teaching and learning of coding with values education and character development. In this way, every child who wishes to can grow to create her own games and apps.

The activity of programming positions the child as an agent, as someone who can make things happen, and as someone with a voice. As the child codes, she develops technical skills and computational thinking. She can problem-solve and deal with abstraction; she can sequence, understand patterns, and use variables and conditionals. However, she must also learn to act with rectitude and become a mensch. In this book, informed by decades of working with children and teachers, I show how the coding playground can become a place to practice: an intentional space to develop a moral compass and character strengths.

I have a sense of urgency. We are educating a generation who will need to put their technical knowledge in conversation with their ethical knowledge. We must start when children are young. Otherwise, we risk growing a new digital divide, in addition to the uneven distribution of access to technology: those who can only think computationally and those who can also act computationally to create a better world and improve their own communities.

My Four Powerful Ideas: A Summary

Throughout the book, I explored the concept of powerful ideas. I discussed how Papert coined the term and how I use it to organize the content and skills we teach in the CAL curriculum. Ideas are mental representations, and they become powerful when we put them to use. The activity of coding enables that transition: from an abstract thought to a concrete action.

I recall my first meeting with Papert in the early 90s. I had recently arrived in Boston from Buenos Aires. I was nervous. I had prepared lots of questions and several sketches of ideas to discuss with him. However, as soon as I got to his office, he told me that we needed to get some groceries he had forgotten. So, our first meeting happened in a supermarket. While choosing tomatoes and cheeses, we were able to more or less engage in a meaningful conversation about ideas.

It was not at all the way I had planned it. I could hardly understand Papert's South African accent, and he probably could not understand my thick Argentinean accent either. I could not show him my diagrams since we were constantly walking the aisles of the supermarket. However, the background noise made it less awkward to ask each other to repeat our sentences several times. It forced us to take the time and pause often. Papert wanted to understand me. I do not think he was interested in getting to know me; he wanted to understand my ideas.

Papert was a man of ideas. I think that he fell in love with computer programming because of its potential to bring about new ideas both at the personal and the societal level. Ideas can change the world. Having grown up under Apartheid, Papert wanted to change the world. I also want to change the world, and I believe that education is one of the best tools to do so. The following are the four powerful ideas that I elaborated in this book. I hope that they will be helpful to others who also believe in the empowering role of new ideas.

- **Coding as a playground:** When engaging children in a computer science learning experience, we welcome play. Through play we can impact all areas of human development: cognitive, socioemotional, language, moral, physical, and even spiritual. The coding playground, in contrast to the coding playpen, promotes opportunities for open-ended exploration, creation of personally meaningful projects, imagination, problem solving, conflict resolution, and collaboration. The coding playground engages children in six behaviors that we can also find in the neighborhood playground: content creation, creativity, choices of conduct, communication, collaboration, and community building. However, for these behaviors to emerge, we need developmentally appropriate tools and pedagogies. When working with young children, it is not enough to borrow programming languages or strategies for middle school or high school. Hence my effort has been focused on creating developmentally appropriate languages such as ScratchJr and KIBO robotics as well as the CAL pedagogy and curriculum. My advice is that when having the choice between technological playgrounds and playpens, choose playgrounds.

- **Coding as another language:** Characterizing coding as a STEM or problem-solving activity is limiting. Instead, if we position the teaching and learning of programming as a new way of thinking and expressing ourselves, we are in the domain of language. Mastering a symbolic system of representation with communicative and expressive functions opens up many opportunities. Learning to code becomes a creative and expressive activity to produce something meaningful and sharable, not only a problem-solving skill set. It has socioemotional implications. The CAL pedagogy promotes the exploration of the similarities and differences between natural and artificial languages for the creation process, their syntax and grammar, and their potential to empower individuals. When coding is taught as a language and not only as STEM, the human dimension comes into play.

- **Coding as a palette of virtues:** Any human activity involves values and making choices to engage in some behaviors and not others. It also involves understanding and taking on responsibilities and consequences. The coding playground provides an intentional opportunity to teach and learn values. The metaphor of a palette of virtues recalls the painter's palette, as opposed to the paint by numbers kit. Like the artist who makes her palette with new colors and mixes and matches them, the coder also has a dynamic virtues palette that is put to use. In the coding playground, ten of these values are explicitly explored: curiosity, perseverance, patience, open-mindedness, optimism, honesty, fairness, generosity, gratitude, and forgiveness. However, new ones can be added. Creative programming can be a pathway for character development and for exploring the socioemotional dimension as well as the ethical dimension of learning. Ultimately, programming helps us to understand that our actions, like the actions of anyone who creates, have consequences.

- **Coding as a bridge:** Programming is a semiotic act that can enable human interactions. It is a meaning-making activity that uses and combines symbols to represent abstract ideas. When we learn to code, we learn a new language. Languages can create or destroy, or they can serve to build bridges or walls. In the coding playground, the intention is to build bridges. CAL proposes that by learning the artificial language of machines, we can also learn the human language that serves us to interact with others, to connect in deep ways, and to craft I–Thou relationships, using Martin Buber's term. Coding can become a bridge, as opposed to a wall that restricts communication and the free exchange of information. The metaphor of coding as a bridge promotes dialogue and meaningful encounters with others. It recognizes the potential of new ways of learning with and about technology to sustain global citizenship in our highly interconnected world with a diversity of local and universal identities and values.

Throughout the book, for each of these four powerful ideas I presented a metaphor contrasting two viewpoints: coding playgrounds versus coding playpens, coding as another language versus coding as STEM, coding as a palette of virtues versus coding as paint by numbers, and coding as a bridge versus coding as a wall. Metaphors shape the way we think and act. As George Lakoff and Mark Johnson's work, *Metaphors We Live By*, showed in the '80s, metaphors might go unnoticed but still structure our most basic understandings of our experiences. My hope is that after you have read through the book, you start to interrogate the role of coding in education and ask yourself how our practices can change as we modify our metaphors.

A Window into Their World: A Diversity of Approaches

It is 2019 and I am sitting in my office. I am navigating the website that features the content produced by the participants in the Beyond STEM project The website is in both English and Spanish, but Arabic and Hebrew are also available. There are pictures of KIBO projects and videos of children and teachers in both Boston and Buenos Aires.

The Beyond STEM project came out of a long-lasting dream I had more than a decade ago: to use programming languages to bring together people from diverse religious and cultural backgrounds, and who speak different natural languages, to learn together. In 2019, the dream became a research project funded by the Templeton World Charity Foundation. In the project, we used KIBO in secular and religious schools, from the three monotheistic faiths (Judaism, Christianity, and Islam), in both Boston and Buenos Aires. Our goal was to understand how robotics can enhance programs with a strong character development component. Each of the eight schools participating in the project would convert their kindergarten classrooms into coding playgrounds. We taught them about KIBO and the CAL pedagogy and curriculum. In the process of coding together, they also learned about each other, their cultures and beliefs, and the ways they approach values education.

On the website, the Colegio Rey Fahd, the Muslim school in Buenos Aires, shares two different projects created by its two kindergarten classrooms. One class chose to adapt the CAL curriculum and focused on the students' experiences as immigrants. The school attracts families from all over the world, and part of its mission is to explore diversity. The class created a beautiful floor map on a giant blue sheet of paper, where painted on the blue spots were continents and in the left-hand corner, the shape of South America. Children decorated and programmed the KIBOs to travel from each of the countries of origin to Argentina (figure 8.2). At the bottom of the map, on a large white shape in children's handwriting, a legend read *Somos un montón de gente, todos diferentes y nos encontramos para aprender a jugar juntos.* In English, this means "We are a lot of people, all different, and we meet to learn and play together."

The second classroom followed the CAL curriculum. The children brainstormed about what made their school special and

Figure 8.2
All the KIBOs made it safely to Argentina

created concrete representations of those things, people, and values. They then placed the representations in a treasure chest in the middle of the room. Divided into teams, the children programmed their KIBOs to move around and create a path to the treasure chest to discover the school treasures.

The teachers at Colegio Cardenal Copello, the Catholic school in Buenos Aires, also followed the CAL curriculum very closely. They focused on the treasures that distinguish the school from others, such as the school badge and uniform, the favorite routines, songs, and games. In teams, students created artwork representing these treasures and placed them into a treasure chest. Each group worked with a KIBO kit to figure out how to program it to move from an assigned corner of the room to the treasure chest so that the treasures could be revealed. Taking advantage of the fact that the children needed to work in large teams due to their large class size, the teachers decided to focus on the values of sharing and collaboration. In their teaching, they reinforced the concept of sharing materials and taking on different roles when working with KIBO.

The Escuela Comunitaria Arlene Fern, the same school I had first worked with robotics and values back in 1998, also stayed close to the CAL curriculum. Differently from other schools, where teaching was done by the kindergarten classroom teaching team, at Arlene Fern the computer science specialist was in charge. Children created and decorated a treasure box, which they placed at the center of the room (figure 8.3). Pairs of students created objects they wanted to put in the treasure box. The objects represented both the students' pride in their school (a school t-shirt, a song, a game, an English book) and their connections to Judaism (a cup used for the ritual blessing over wine, candles, flowers). KIBO's job was to deliver the objects to the treasure chest. Students learned to program KIBO to take different paths and explored different ways to attach the objects to the robots so they could be safely delivered. Most of them ended up using the KIBO art platforms as carrying devices.

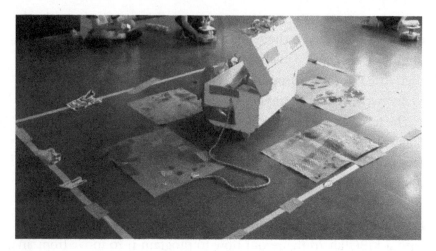

Figure 8.3
Escuela Comunitaria Arlene Fern treasure chest

The public school in Buenos Aires, JIN E DE 17 Juana Manso, had two participating kindergarten classrooms. In one, they adapted the CAL curriculum so students could revisit all past projects done throughout the year and identify connections to the school's values. Working in collaboration with the arts teacher and the librarian, the classroom teachers created a giant maze populated with the different projects. Students programmed KIBO to take a tour through the maze, explore all of the projects, and choose the ones they wanted to take back to the treasure chest. That is, students had to decide which of the projects best represented the values of their school community to be kept in the treasure chest. In addition, this classroom chose to place a GoPro camera atop one of the KIBOs so the students could experience a "KIBO eye view" of the route the robots took.

The second classroom also worked with the CAL curriculum but chose to focus on the value of environmentalism, which they had been exploring throughout the year. They transformed KIBO into a guardian of nature and gave it a friend named KIBA. They created two dolls with recyclable material and placed them atop KIBO and

KIBA. They then programmed the robots to travel to various elements of nature including trees, fish, and others, which they had carefully created in their classroom, to protect them.

Unlike the projects from the Buenos Aires schools, the projects from the Boston schools did not closely follow the CAL curriculum. Teachers felt more comfortable adapting it, maybe because most of them had previous KIBO experience. The schools in Boston were also smaller and had smaller class sizes, and thus, the size of the groups of children working with KIBO was also smaller.

At Al Bustan/Malik Academy in Boston, the students begin learning about God and the Quran as soon as they start kindergarten. This is very different than what happens at Colegio Rey Fahd in Buenos Aires, in which religion is almost absent in the kindergarten curriculum. At Al Bustan, the teachers used the KIBO final project as an opportunity to deepen the children's understanding of Islam. The students were taught a popular song called *"Rahman ya Rahman,"* which talks about connecting with God through the Quran and filling our hearts with the words of God. They then choreographed a dance to the song to perform alongside the KIBOs. As the students stepped forward and clapped in their dance, the KIBOs moved forward and waited for their claps and then they all moved backward. This song was both an opportunity to engage with the Arabic language and with some of the major tenets of their faith. It also brought dance and movement to the coding playground. The KIBOs were not decorated, and art materials were not integrated into the project because according to Islam, there cannot be pictorial representations of God.

In preparing the dance, the students came up with many questions, like "Who is Allah? How can He see us, but we can't see Him?" The teachers chose to follow the student's lead and extended the final project to grapple with the concept of God. They read the book *Ilyas and Duck Search for Allah* by Omar S. Khawaja and the children acted it out together with KIBO: one little girl played Ilyas, and KIBO was programmed to play Duck. Together, they made their way through different parts of the classroom searching for Allah, before ultimately understanding that God is everywhere.

Our Lady's Academy in Boston took the final project in a different direction. As a Catholic school, they work with nine virtues: faith, love, kindness, generosity, courage, honesty, respect, responsibility, and humility. Each month, a student from each classroom is acknowledged for displaying one of those traits, and each day the teachers conduct their classes with these virtues in mind. They created a virtues parade in which KIBOs marched together. Each pair of students chose one of the nine school virtues, created a flag for that virtue, and attached it to a balloon carried by a KIBO. To integrate the literacy component, they read *Clifford and the Big Parade* by Norman Bridwell and *Balloons over Broadway* by Melissa Sweet. Every student was given two small squares of paper. At the top of each was one of the school's virtues, and beneath it was a blank space for them to draw a representation of what that virtue meant to them. One student drew herself helping collect potatoes for a Thanksgiving food drive, showing humility. Another drew herself and her classmates walking into the school chapel, showing faith. One boy drew a picture of himself and his "girlfriend," showing love.

At the JCDS in Boston, students programmed the robots to travel a student-made landscape of Israel as the song *"Eretz Yisrael Sheli"* ("My Land of Israel") played in the background. Throughout the CAL curriculum, teachers integrated KIBO with Hebrew language education. The final project was a culmination of that integration and the collaboration between the different members of the teaching team: a lead teacher who was Jewish and spoke minimal Hebrew, an Israeli teacher who was responsible for the Hebrew language immersion, and a non-Jewish STEM teacher who partnered with the lead classroom teachers throughout the day.

Students shared the final projects with the larger community, and the multipurpose room in the school was converted into an exhibit room. Family and friends were invited to come see KIBO travel through the Israel landscape. After the formal presentation, which included children singing and dancing to the song, visitors were handed a sheet of questions to discuss with the children. During this interactive part of the exhibit, visitors asked questions and students explained the design process, decision points, successes and frustrations, and, fundamentally, how to program KIBO.

The secular school in Boston, the Eliot-Pearson Children's School (EPCS), is the lab school of the Department of Child Study and Human Development at Tufts University. The school chose to work on two final projects. For the first one, they programmed the KIBO robots to dance and light up as the song "This Little Light of Mine" played in the background. The students used repeat loops to make KIBO dance to the song and programmed the lightbulbs to light up at every "I'm gonna let it shine" line. The choice of this beloved children's tune, which is a spiritual song transformed by the US civil rights movement into an anthem of solidarity and power, is interesting at a secular school. The lyrics repeat, "Everywhere I go, Lord, I'm gonna let it shine. Let it shine, let it shine, let it shine!" That said, the song, which became a celebration of the light within the self, embodies the values of EPCS, a school that focuses on anti-bias education, acceptance, and the celebration of individuality. The song was used to teach the concept of repeat loops but also to facilitate discussion about the school's values.

The second project was closely aligned with the CAL curriculum and the treasure chest idea. Following an extended discussion about the different characteristics of their school, the students engaged in drawing and writing cards about their favorite school treasures. At the end of the class, the teacher collected the cards and placed them in a treasure chest for safe keeping. The final project then emerged out of a game the teachers led. "Someone broke into the chest and took out all the treasures and hid them in different parts of the classroom," explained the teachers. "We need to program KIBOs to travel through the different obstacles in our classrooms, to find the treasures, and return them to the chest." In a clever way, EPCS teachers took the CAL curriculum and made it into a game.

As I navigate the Beyond STEM project website and read the stories of the different KIBO projects in the eight schools, I see that each found a unique way to integrate the teaching of robotics and values. I see creativity in children's projects but also in the teacher's adaptations of the CAL curriculum. I admire how the teachers tailored their KIBO time to emphasize different cultural and religious traditions. I learned about how each of the schools chose to display their palette of virtues, and I see the particulars and the universals. I am amazed by the diversity of approaches and configurations of the teaching teams.

I see coding playgrounds in which students developed computational thinking, coding, and problem-solving skills. We conducted coding assessments and found that an overwhelming number of kindergartners, 75 percent of the students in the sample, reached the top two levels of knowledge, skills, and understanding at the end of the curriculum. The children were curious, determined, and persistent. We discovered that they deeply engaged with the values in the palette of virtues. They learned to take turns, collaborate, and share classroom resources while developing patience, generosity, and gratitude. They were forgiving to themselves, others, and their teachers, and they brought optimism and fairness to their work with KIBO. Across the city and across the globe, the learning of a programming language provided a powerful venue to explore the universality and the particularities of bringing values into the coding playground.

On the website, I see comments that teachers wrote to one another. The original idea was to hold a final virtual synchronous conference for all teachers in both Buenos Aires and Boston to come together and share their learning. However, due to the lack of a shared language and logistical difficulties regarding the project's timing, this was not possible. Instead, we conducted two final meetings in Buenos Aires and in Boston.

In those meetings I learned that some teachers reported that for their young students, it was easier to understand why a school of a different faith focused their final KIBO project around a song, book, or value they were not familiar with rather than understand the cross-continental differences within faith communities. For example, when the kindergarten students at the Jewish day school in Boston watched the video of the Jewish day school in Buenos Aires, they were delighted to see the kids in blue and white (the colors of the Israeli flag). But they were quite confused as to why the Jewish children were talking in Spanish, a language they did not associate with Judaism. To the adult viewer, this detail goes unnoticed.

Similarly, while the Muslim schools in Boston and in Buenos Aires include Arabic in their instruction, the final project video from Boston showcased a variety of accents as the children sang and danced with KIBO to a popular devotional song about Allah. For some of the children in Buenos Aires, who came from countries with different Arabic dialects, the different accents were noticeable. The idea that there are different Muslim communities around the world was made tangible through this experience.

The Beyond STEM project was borne from a dream I had long time ago. Despite the project's success, its implementation was not exactly what I dreamed. We were not able to take teachers and children to visit each other's schools, nor could we have more time to learn from each other or include families in the work. However, one story from the final meeting with all the Boston teachers showed me the potential of this kind of work to build bridges. The teachers from Al Bustan explained to the group the importance of the song they chose for the final KIBO project. "Allah is at the heart of everything that happens in the world. The job of the young child, who is not yet, in Muslim tradition, responsible for formal liturgy or text study, is to notice the world around her and think about Allah," explained one of the teachers.

Immediately, the Israeli Hebrew teacher from JCDS raised her hand and asked the name of the book. The teachers from Al Bustan told her the name hesitantly, "It's about Allah." In other words, it is a Muslim book. The Israeli teacher seemed unphased and said, "I love it. I want to teach it. I have another book I think you might like, *Abraham in Search of God.*" The exchange was powerful. A modern Jewish Israeli teacher sharing books to teach about God's presence in the world with a religious Muslim teacher in hijab. These were not teachers interested in interfaith work. They participated in the project because they wanted to bring robotics and computational thinking to their classrooms, yet the coding playground provided an opportunity to engage in a meaningful dialogue that would never have otherwise occurred. Borrowing Buber's language, through the It of the KIBO, they were able to engage in an I–Thou encounter.

Further Readings

This book focuses on my own work, first as a graduate student at the MIT Media Lab and then, for the last twenty years, as a professor at Tufts University and director of the DevTech Research Group. However, my research draws on ideas, projects, and studies conducted by many people in many places over a long span of time. You can find those citations in peer-reviewed papers I have published in the past, which are linked on my website: http://www.tufts.edu/~mbers01/.

In addition to the materials cited in the text, I chose a small subset of books with powerful ideas that have inspired my thinking and my writing for the making of this book.

Bruner, Jerome. *Child's Talk: Learning to Use Language*. New York: W. W. Norton & Company, 1983.

Buber, Martin. *I and Thou*. New York: Scribner, 1958.

Csikszentmihalyi, Mihaly. *Flow: The Psychology of Optimal Experience*. New York: HarperCollins, 2000.

Dehaene, Stanislas. *Reading in the Brain: The New Science of How We Read*. New York: Penguin, 2009.

Duckworth, Angela. *Grit: The Power of Passion and Perseverance*. New York: Scribner, 2016.

Ford, Aníbal. *Navegaciones: Comunicación, Cultura y Crisis*. Buenos Aires: Amorrortu, 1994.

Gilligan, Carol. *In a Different Voice*. Cambridge: Harvard University Press, 1982.

Goody, J. *The Logic of Writing and the Organization of Society* (Studies in Literacy, the Family, Culture and the State). Cambridge: Cambridge University Press, 1986.

Kohlberg, Lawrence. *The Philosophy of Moral Development: Moral Stages and the Idea of Justice*. San Francisco: Harper & Row, 1981.

Lave, Jean, and Wenger, Etienne. *Situated Learning: Legitimate Peripheral Participation*. Cambridge, England: Cambridge University Press, 1991.

Lerner, Richard. *The Good Teen*. New York: Three Rivers Press, 2007.

Ong, Walter J. *Orality and Literacy: The Technologizing of the Word*. London: Methuen, 1982.

Papert, Seymour. *Mindstorms: Children, Computers, and Powerful Ideas*. New York: Basic Books, 1980.

Papert, Seymour. *The Children's Machine: Rethinking School in the Age of the Computer*. New York: Basic Books, 1993.

Piscitelli, Alejandro. *Ciberculturas 2.0. En la Era de las Máquinas Inteligentes*, Buenos Aires, Argentina: Paidos, 2002.

Resnick, Mitchel. *Lifelong Kindergarten: Cultivating Creativity through Projects, Passions, Peers, and Play*. Cambridge: The MIT Press, 2017.

Turkle, Sherry. *The Second Self: Computers and the Human Spirit*. New York: Basic Books, 1984.

Turkle, Sherry. *Reclaiming Conversation: The Power of Talk in a Digital Age*. New York: Penguin Press, 2015.

Vee, Annette. *Coding Literacy: How Computer Programming Is Changing Writing*. Cambridge: The MIT Press, 2017.

Vygotsky, Lev S. *Mind in Society: The Development of Higher Psychological Processes*. Cambridge: Harvard University Press, 1978.

Wolf, Maryanne. *Proust and the Squid: The Story and Science of the Reading Brain*. New York: HarperCollins, 2007.

Resources

For links to videos, projects, curriculum materials, teaching tools, and other resources related to the work mentioned in this book, please visit the website of my DevTech Research Group at Tufts University: https://sites.tufts.edu/devtech/.

Seymour Papert warned us again about *technocentrism*, which he described as the fallacy of referring all questions to technology. If and when you visit the DevTech website, you might be tempted to spend time browsing information about ScratchJr and KIBO and the many videos of different experiences done in classrooms all over the world. However, there are other less shiny and appealing elements that still make a coding playground possible. Please make sure to also find them.

Curriculum

We have developed over twenty free curricular units that integrate the teaching of coding, robotics, and computational thinking through both ScratchJr and KIBO, with diverse subjects such as literacy, math, social sciences, geography, and Judaic studies.

All of the units are developmentally appropriate for children ages four through eight and are aligned with the coding as a playground philosophy that engages the cognitive as well as the socioemotional dimensions of learning. The units provide opportunities for promoting the six Cs or positive behaviors of the PTD framework through plugged and unplugged activities that use movement, song, and arts and crafts. In addition, the curriculum is designed to encourage the development and practice of the character strengths in the palette of virtues.

Three of our curricular units have been widely used, evaluated, and improved over the years. Make sure you check them out:

- The Coding as Another Language (CAL) curriculum for both KIBO and ScratchJr that integrates literacy: https://sites.tufts.edu/codingasanotherlanguage/.
- The Dances Around the World curriculum for KIBO that integrates social sciences: https://sites.tufts.edu/devtech/files/2018/03/KIBOCurriculum_DancesAroundtheWorld.pdf.
- The Limudei Code-esh series for both KIBO and ScratchJr that integrates Jewish studies through six different holidays: http://sites.tufts.edu/devtech/jewish-curricula-series/.

Positive Technological Development Tools

PTD is a theoretical framework that guides the design and evaluation of curriculum, teaching resources, and technologies to specifically address six behaviors: content creation, creativity, communication, collaboration, choices of conduct, and community building. We have created a set of free PTD tools to help teachers, researchers, and designers implement PTD in their own work:

- PTD cards: A set of cards with games and instructions to foster discussion among adults who plan to bring technology into a learning setting for children. The cards can be printed back-to-back, cut out, and used in the collaborative, interactive evaluation of technological tools or technology-rich learning setting.

- PTD engagement checklists: Two different rubrics serve to evaluate if the six Cs of PTD are happening. The first can be used to assess if children are developing these behaviors; the other can be used to evaluate the learning environment and the teacher/facilitator.

These can be found here: http://sites.tufts.edu/devtech/ptd/.

Assessments

We have developed different ways to evaluate if children are learning to code in expressive ways and develop computational thinking. In classrooms with scarce resources, children tend to share robots and tablets; therefore, the final projects do not always present the result of an individual learning experience but rather the progress of a group. Hence, we developed assessment tools that can be used to evaluate both the final project and an individual's learning progression:

- **Final project rubric:** This easy-to-use tool serves to assess the complexity and creativity demonstrated by the final KIBO and ScratchJr project and places them on a one to five continuum: budding, developing, proficient, advanced, and distinguished. Rubric evaluation criteria include complexity of programming concepts, block variety, purposefulness, and elaboration. The rubric can be used by both researchers and educators and includes specific guidelines for scoring.

- **TechCheck:** This is a validated, unplugged assessment used to evaluate computational thinking in children. TechCheck presents children with logical tasks that do not require prior coding knowledge and can thus be used not only in teaching but also in research studies that employ a control group. The assessment contains multiple choice questions that can be administered to individuals, whole classrooms, or groups in an average of twelve minutes.

- **Coding stages assessment (CSA):** This tool evaluates the coding stage in which a child fits in with respect to KIBO and ScratchJr. Its format requires prior knowledge of the coding tool. CSA consists of open-ended questions and can take ten to forty-five minutes, depending on the child's knowledge. The assessment begins with questions from the early most stages and only progresses to later stage questions if the child has sufficiently answered the prior set.

Professional Development Opportunities

On the DevTech website, you will find many opportunities for both online and face-to-face professional development. These trainings focus not only on KIBO and/or ScratchJr but also on the powerful ideas discussed in this book. In addition, if you are interested in different kinds of training opportunities, please do not hesitate to contact me.